IoT And Multimedia Technology

Priya Lakshmi S. | Shanmughaa Priyaa R. | Shanmugha Prabha P.

KHANNA BOOK PUBLISHING CO. (P) Ltd.
4C/4344, Ansari Road, Darya Ganj,
New Delhi, India

Sathyabama Institute of Science and Technology
Jeppiaar Nagar, Rajiv Gandhi Salai,
Chennai, Tamilnadu, India

Dear Readers,

To prevent the piracy, this book is secured with HIGH SECURITY HOLOGRAM on the front title cover. In case you don't find the hologram on the front cover title, please write us to at contact@khannabooks.com or whatsapp us at +91-99109 09320 and avail special gift voucher for yourself.

Specimen of Hologram on front Cover title:

Moreover, there is a SPECIAL DISCOUNT COUPON for you with EVERY HOLOGRAM.

How to avail this SPECIAL DISCOUNT:

Step 1: Scratch the hologram
Step 2: Under the scratch area, your "coupon code" is available
Step 3: Logon to www.khannabooks.com
Step 4: Use your "coupon code" in the shopping cart and get your copy at a special discount
Step 5: Enjoy your reading!

Thanks,
Khanna Publishing House

ISBN: 978-93-55383-68-6

IoT And Multimedia Technology
by **Priya Lakshmi S.;**
Shanmughaa Priyaa R.;
Shanmugha Prabha P.

First Edition: 2025
Reprint: 2026

To view complete list of books, please scan the QR Code:

Published by:
Khanna Book Publishing Co. (P) Ltd.
CIN: U22110DL1998PTC095547

Visit us at: www.khannabooks.com
Write us at: contact@khannabooks.com

Printed in Bharat.

Preface

The convergence of the Internet of Things (IoT) and multimedia technology is transforming the digital landscape, enabling seamless communication, intelligent data processing, and innovative applications across various industries. As IoT continues to evolve, its integration with multimedia systems is redefining fields such as healthcare, smart cities, entertainment, and industrial automation. This book serves as a comprehensive guide to explore the intricate connection between IoT and multimedia communication, offering a profound understanding of their interconnected evolution and far-reaching impact.

This book offers a thorough examination of fundamental principles and real-world applications in IoT and multimedia communication. It explores key areas such as network protocols, data transmission methodologies, embedded systems, and real-time multimedia processing. With a structured approach that balances theory and application, this book presents key concepts through case studies, industry examples, and practical insights. Readers will gain a comprehensive understanding of how multimedia technology enhances IoT ecosystems, fostering efficiency, scalability, and enriched user experiences.

We hope this book serves as a valuable resource for those eager to explore the evolving landscape of IoT and multimedia communication. Whether you are an academic, a technology enthusiast, or an industry professional, this book offers essential knowledge and valuable perspectives to help you navigate and make meaningful contributions to this rapidly advancing field.

Contents

UNIT 1

Multimedia Big Data in IoT Ecosystems

1.1 INTRODUCTION TO MULTIMEDIA BIG DATA IN IOT ECOSYSTEMS

The exponential growth of Internet of Things (IoT) devices has fundamentally transformed the landscape of data generation, processing, and analytics. While early IoT deployments primarily focused on scalar sensor data, contemporary IoT ecosystems are increasingly characterized by the proliferation of multimedia data streams. By 2030, IoT device deployments are projected to exceed 125 billion globally, with a significant proportion generating rich multimedia content including images, audio, video, and complex multimodal data.

Multimedia Big Data (MMBD) in IoT environments presents unique characteristics that distinguish it from traditional big data paradigms. These include:

- **Heterogeneity**: MMBD encompasses diverse data formats (images, videos, audio, text) with varying structures, resolutions, and quality levels.
- **Human-centricity**: Much of the multimedia data is generated through human interactions or is intended for human consumption, introducing semantic complexity.
- **Multimodality**: Information is often distributed across multiple modalities, requiring sophisticated integration techniques.
- **Scale**: The volume and velocity of multimedia data significantly exceed that of scalar sensor data, imposing substantial demands on storage, processing, and transmission infrastructure.

The convergence of Multimedia Big Data and IoT creates a symbiotic relationship, where advances in one domain catalyze innovation in the other. IoT provides the sensory infrastructure for capturing multimedia data at unprecedented scale, while MMBD analytics enable IoT systems to derive actionable insights from complex, unstructured information streams.

This chapter explores the multifaceted challenges, architectural considerations, and transformative applications emerging at the intersection of Multimedia Big Data Computing and IoT. We examine the technical foundations, current limitations, and promising research directions in this rapidly evolving field.

1.2 FOUNDATIONAL FRAMEWORK FOR MULTIMEDIA BIG DATA IN IOT

The lifecycle of multimedia big data in IoT encompasses several interconnected phases, each with unique requirements and challenges:

1. **Data Acquisition**: Capturing multimedia content through various IoT sensors and devices, including cameras, microphones, wearables, and specialized multimedia sensors.
2. **Data Processing**: Transforming raw multimedia data through compression, encoding, filtering, and feature extraction to prepare it for analysis.
3. **Data Storage**: Implementing efficient storage solutions that balance accessibility, security, and cost-effectiveness for massive multimedia datasets.
4. **Data Dissemination**: Distributing processed multimedia content across networks to relevant stakeholders and systems.
5. **Data Presentation**: Rendering multimedia content in forms that maximize human interpretability and decision support.

The IoT infrastructure significantly impacts each phase of this lifecycle, introducing both opportunities and constraints. Edge computing capabilities enable preliminary processing of multimedia data at the point of collection, reducing bandwidth requirements and latency. Fog computing extends this processing capability to the network edge, providing intermediate analytics before data reaches centralized cloud infrastructure.

Distinctive Challenges of Multimedia Big Data in IoT

The management and analysis of multimedia big data in IoT environments face several distinctive challenges:

Real-time Processing Constraints

IoT applications frequently require near-instantaneous processing of multimedia streams to enable timely decision-making. For example, smart traffic management systems must analyze video feeds in real-time to detect congestion, accidents, or traffic violations. This necessitates efficient algorithms capable of extracting meaningful insights from high-dimensional multimedia data within strict temporal constraints.

Unstructured and Multimodal Data Complexity

Unlike structured numerical data, multimedia content in IoT is predominantly unstructured and often multimodal. A smart healthcare system might simultaneously process audio recordings of patient speech, video of physical movements, and physiological sensor readings. Integrating these diverse data modalities to derive coherent insights presents significant technical challenges.

Perception and Understanding Complexity

Multimedia data often contains high-level semantic information that requires sophisticated interpretation. For instance, understanding the context, emotions, and activities depicted in a video stream from a smart home camera necessitates advanced computer vision and pattern recognition capabilities.

Scalability and Efficiency Concerns

The volume and velocity of multimedia data in IoT far exceed that of traditional sensor data. A single high-definition video camera can generate several gigabytes of data per hour, while a network of such cameras can produce petabytes daily. This scale demands highly efficient processing, storage, and transmission solutions.

1.3 ENERGY CONSERVATION: A CRITICAL CHALLENGE IN MULTIMEDIA IOT

The Energy Consumption Dilemma

Energy consumption represents one of the most significant constraints for multimedia big data processing in IoT environments. The energy-intensive nature of multimedia data acquisition, processing, and transmission poses particular challenges for battery-powered and resource-constrained IoT devices. This section examines the multifaceted aspects of energy conservation in multimedia IoT systems.

Power Depletion Factors in Multimedia IoT

Multiple factors contribute to energy consumption in multimedia IoT systems:

- **Data Acquisition**: Capturing high-resolution multimedia content requires substantial energy, particularly for video recording or continuous audio monitoring.
- **Local Processing**: Performing even basic preprocessing of multimedia data (e.g., compression, feature extraction) demands significant computational resources and corresponding energy.
- **Data Transmission**: Wireless transmission of multimedia content is particularly energy-intensive, with energy consumption often scaling with data volume.
- **Storage Operations**: Writing and reading multimedia data to/from storage media consumes power, which is particularly relevant for edge devices with local storage capabilities.

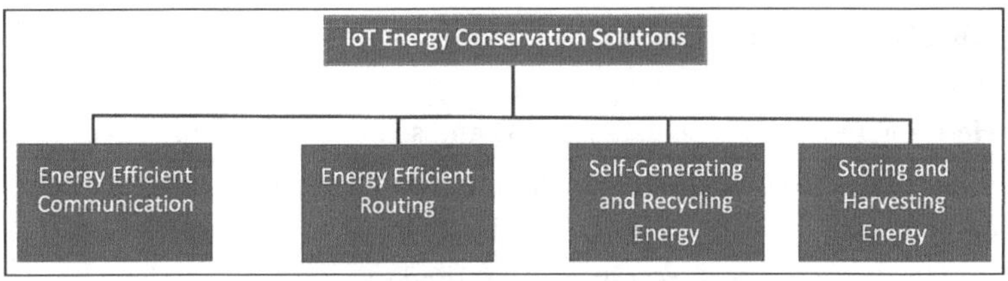

Figure 1.1: Energy Conservation Solutions

Energy Efficiency Approaches and Technologies

Several approaches have emerged to address energy conservation in multimedia IoT:

Energy-Efficient Communication Protocols

Specialized communication protocols designed for multimedia IoT traffic optimize transmission efficiency while maintaining quality of service. Techniques such as adaptive compression, selective transmission, and priority-based scheduling help reduce the energy footprint of multimedia data communication.

Energy Harvesting and Self-Sustaining Systems

Energy harvesting technologies enable IoT devices to generate power from environmental sources such as solar, thermal, kinetic, or RF energy. These approaches are particularly valuable for remote multimedia sensors that cannot rely on continuous external power sources.

Cross-Layer Energy Optimization

Modifications to the protocol stack of communication technologies can significantly enhance energy efficiency. Cross-layer optimization approaches that consider application requirements, network conditions, and device capabilities can dynamically adjust operational parameters to minimize energy consumption.

Energy-Efficient IoT (EEIoT): Emerging Paradigms

The concept of "Green IoT" represents a holistic approach to energy conservation across multiple dimensions:

- **Service Management**: Optimizing service delivery to minimize resource utilization while maintaining quality of service.
- **Heterogeneous Communication**: Selecting the most energy-efficient communication medium based on data characteristics and network conditions.
- **Physical Environment Integration**: Leveraging environmental context to optimize device operation and data collection strategies.
- **Sensor-Cloud Integration**: Balancing processing load between sensor nodes and cloud infrastructure to minimize overall energy consumption.

1.4 ARCHITECTURAL FOUNDATIONS FOR REAL-TIME MULTIMEDIA DATA STREAM MONITORING

Architectural Requirements for Multimedia IoT Streams

Effective processing of multimedia data streams in IoT environments requires architectures specifically designed to address their unique characteristics:

- **High Data Velocity**: Continuous streams of multimedia data arriving at varying rates.
- **Heterogeneity**: Diverse data formats and structures from multiple sensor types.
- **Low Latency Requirements**: Many applications require near-real-time processing and response.
- **Scalability**: Architecture must accommodate growing numbers of devices and increasing data rates.
- **Fault Tolerance**: Robust operation despite potential device failures or network interruptions.

Layered Architectural Approaches

Multimedia IoT architectures typically adopt a layered approach:

Sensing Layer

This foundation layer encompasses the diverse multimedia sensors responsible for data acquisition. It includes various devices such as cameras, microphones, specialized sensors, and increasingly, multisensory platforms that combine multiple modalities. Key considerations at this layer include sensor calibration, energy efficiency, and initial data filtering.

Network Layer

The network layer facilitates the transmission of multimedia data from sensors to processing infrastructure. This layer must address challenges related to bandwidth constraints, quality of service, and heterogeneous network technologies. Adaptive transmission protocols that optimize based on network conditions and data criticality are essential for efficient operation.

Processing Layer

The processing layer encompasses the computational infrastructure responsible for analyzing multimedia streams. Modern architectures distribute processing across multiple tiers:

- **Edge Processing**: Preliminary analysis at or near the data source, such as feature extraction or event detection.
- **Fog Processing**: Intermediate processing at network edge nodes, enabling aggregation and correlation across multiple streams.
- **Cloud Processing**: Comprehensive analytics leveraging the computational power and storage capacity of cloud infrastructure.

Data Stream Management Systems for Multimedia IoT

Data Stream Management Systems (DSMS) play a crucial role in handling continuous multimedia data flows in IoT environments. Unlike traditional database management systems designed for persistent data, DSMS are optimized for processing transient data streams. Key capabilities include:

- **Continuous Query Processing**: Executing standing queries over data streams rather than finite datasets.
- **Window-Based Operations**: Processing data within defined temporal or count-based windows.
- **Adaptive Query Optimization**: Dynamically adjusting processing strategies based on stream characteristics and system load.
- **Load Shedding**: Selectively discarding data during peak loads to maintain system performance.

Semantic Understanding through Ontologies

Ontologies enable semantic interpretation of multimedia streams, providing a formal representation of domain knowledge that facilitates more sophisticated analysis. In IoT contexts, ontologies can:

- **Enhance Interoperability**: Providing a common semantic framework across heterogeneous devices and data sources.
- **Support Context Awareness**: Incorporating contextual information to improve interpretation of multimedia content.

- **Enable Reasoning**: Supporting inference mechanisms that can derive implicit information from explicit observations.
- **Facilitate Discovery**: Enabling semantic search and discovery of relevant multimedia content.

1.5 DEEP LEARNING FOR MULTIMEDIA ANALYTICS IN IOT

Limitations of Traditional Analytics for Multimedia IoT

Traditional data analytics approaches face significant limitations when applied to multimedia IoT data:

- **Structural Constraints**: Conventional database systems are ill-suited for unstructured multimedia content.
- **Feature Complexity**: Manual feature engineering is impractical for the high-dimensional space of multimedia data.
- **Scalability Issues**: Traditional algorithms often fail to scale effectively with the volume of multimedia IoT data.
- **Dynamic Nature**: The non-stationary characteristics of IoT data streams challenge static analysis models.

Deep Learning Paradigms for Multimedia IoT

Deep learning offers compelling advantages for multimedia IoT analytics through its capacity to:

- **Automatically Extract Features**: Hierarchical feature learning eliminates the need for manual feature engineering.
- **Handle Multimodal Data**: Specialized architectures can integrate information across different modalities.
- **Scale Efficiently**: Parallelizable architectures can leverage GPU acceleration for processing massive datasets.
- **Adapt to Non-Stationarity**: Online learning approaches can continuously refine models as data characteristics evolve.

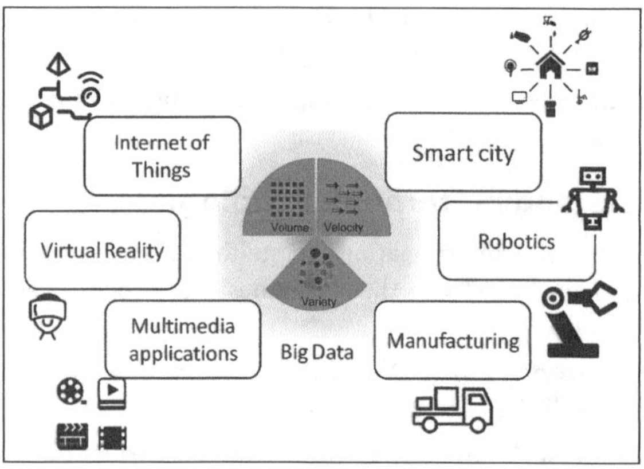

Figure 1.2: Deep Learning for Iot

Deep Learning Architectures for Multimedia Analysis

Several deep learning architectures have demonstrated particular efficacy for multimedia IoT applications:

Convolutional Neural Networks (CNNs)

CNNs excel at visual pattern recognition tasks, making them ideal for processing image and video data from IoT cameras. Applications include:

- **Object Detection and Recognition**: Identifying and classifying objects in smart city surveillance cameras.
- **Scene Understanding**: Interpreting complex visual scenes in autonomous vehicles.
- **Anomaly Detection**: Identifying unusual patterns in visual data streams from industrial IoT deployments.

Recurrent Neural Networks (RNNs) and LSTM Networks

RNNs and their variants are particularly effective for sequential data, including:

- **Audio Analysis**: Processing speech and sound in smart home environments.
- **Temporal Pattern Recognition**: Identifying patterns in time-series multimedia data from wearable devices.
- **Predictive Modeling**: Forecasting future states based on historical multimedia streams.

Deep Autoencoders

Autoencoders provide powerful tools for:

- **Dimensionality Reduction**: Compressing high-dimensional multimedia features.
- **Noise Reduction**: Cleaning multimedia signals from low-quality IoT sensors.
- **Anomaly Detection**: Identifying unusual patterns in multimedia streams.

Implementation Challenges and Optimization Strategies

While deep learning offers powerful capabilities for multimedia IoT analytics, its implementation faces several challenges:

- **Computational Demands**: Training deep models requires substantial computational resources, often exceeding the capabilities of IoT devices.
- **Energy Constraints**: The energy requirements of deep learning inference can strain battery-powered IoT devices.
- **Latency Requirements**: Many IoT applications require low-latency analytics incompatible with complex model evaluation.
- **Limited Labeled Data**: Obtaining annotated multimedia data for supervised learning can be costly and time-consuming.

To address these challenges, several optimization strategies have emerged:

- **Model Compression**: Techniques such as pruning, quantization, and knowledge distillation reduce model size and computational requirements.

- **Federated Learning**: Distributing model training across devices while keeping data local addresses privacy concerns and reduces communication overhead.
- **Transfer Learning**: Leveraging pre-trained models reduces the need for large, labeled datasets and accelerates training.
- **Neuromorphic Computing**: Specialized hardware architectures inspired by biological neural systems offer energy-efficient processing for deep learning models.

1.6 APPLICATIONS AND CASE STUDIES

Smart Cities and Urban Surveillance

Multimedia IoT deployments in smart cities enable comprehensive urban monitoring and management:

- **Traffic Management**: Video analytics from traffic cameras optimize signal timing, detect incidents, and manage congestion.
- **Public Safety**: Acoustic sensors detect gunshots or anomalous sounds, while cameras identify suspicious activities.
- **Environmental Monitoring**: Multimedia sensors track air quality, noise pollution, and urban microclimate conditions.

Case Study: Barcelona's integrated multimedia IoT platform combines video, audio, and environmental sensors to optimize urban resource allocation, reducing traffic congestion by 21% and lowering urban noise pollution by 30% in monitored areas.

Healthcare and Remote Patient Monitoring

Multimedia IoT transforms healthcare delivery through:

- **Remote Diagnostics**: Video and audio analysis enable preliminary diagnosis without physical consultation.
- **Continuous Monitoring**: Wearable devices with multimedia capabilities track patient activity, sleep patterns, and physiological responses.
- **Rehabilitation Support**: Computer vision systems monitor exercise form and progress during home rehabilitation.

Case Study: A remote patient monitoring system for stroke rehabilitation integrates wearable sensors with video analytics to assess movement quality, resulting in 40% improved recovery rates compared to traditional home rehabilitation approaches.

Smart Agriculture and Environmental Monitoring

Multimedia IoT applications in agriculture include:

- **Crop Health Assessment**: Multispectral imaging detects plant stress, disease, and nutrient deficiencies.
- **Livestock Monitoring**: Computer vision and audio analysis track animal behavior, health, and welfare.
- **Pest and Disease Detection**: Automated visual inspection identifies early signs of pest infestation or crop disease.

- **Case Study:** An integrated multimedia monitoring system for vineyard management combines thermal imaging, visual analysis, and environmental sensing to optimize irrigation, reducing water usage by 30% while increasing crop quality.

Industrial IoT and Manufacturing

In industrial environments, multimedia IoT enables:

- **Quality Control**: Automated visual inspection detects product defects with greater accuracy than human inspection.
- **Predictive Maintenance**: Acoustic and vibration analysis identifies early signs of equipment failure.
- **Process Optimization**: Thermal imaging and visual monitoring identify inefficiencies in manufacturing processes.

Case Study: An automotive manufacturing facility implemented a multimedia IoT quality control system that reduced defect rates by 64% through the integration of high-speed cameras, acoustic sensors, and deep learning-based analysis.

1.7 FUTURE RESEARCH DIRECTIONS AND EMERGING TRENDS

Multimodal Deep Learning for Heterogeneous Data Integration

Future research will increasingly focus on integrating information across multiple modalities to derive comprehensive insights. Approaches that combine vision, audio, and sensor data through attention mechanisms and cross-modal learning represent promising directions for multimedia IoT analytics.

Edge Intelligence for Real-Time Multimedia Processing

Advances in edge computing hardware and optimized deep learning models will enable more sophisticated analytics at the network edge. This trend will reduce latency, bandwidth requirements, and privacy concerns associated with centralized processing of sensitive multimedia data.

Quantum Computing for Multimedia Big Data

Quantum computing offers transformative potential for processing massive multimedia datasets. Quantum algorithms for pattern recognition, dimensionality reduction, and optimization could dramatically accelerate multimedia analytics for IoT applications.

Human-Centric Interpretable Multimedia Analytics

As multimedia IoT systems increasingly influence critical decisions, ensuring interpretability and explainability of AI-driven insights becomes essential. Research into visualization techniques, attention mechanisms, and narrative generation from multimedia analytics will enhance human understanding and trust.

Privacy-Preserving Multimedia Analytics

The sensitive nature of multimedia data in many IoT deployments (e.g., healthcare, home monitoring) necessitates robust privacy protections. Emerging approaches such as federated learning, differential privacy, and homomorphic encryption offer promising avenues for privacy-preserving multimedia analytics.

SUMMARY

Multimedia Big Data Computing for IoT pays attention to the management and analysis of massive multimedia data from numerous interconnected devices for increased efficiency and performance. One key example is intelligent data processing in energy conservation, which optimizes power usage in IoT frameworks. Yet the fusion of Multimedia Big Data Computing with IoT has serious problems regarding data security, scalability, and time constraints. In solving these issues, there has to be a clear structure for monitoring the real-time data streams to facilitate prompt data collection, analysis, and decision making. Deep learning is significant in dealing with multimedia data in IoT since it provides more sophisticated techniques for pattern recognition, predictive analysis, and general automation. With advanced deep learning techniques, IoT frameworks will effectively utilize large volumes of multimedia data, which will result in better-performing and smarter applications in different sectors.

2

UNIT

Guaranteed Service Model

2.1 INTRODUCTION

The proliferation of Internet of Things (IoT) devices has ushered in a new era of data generation and transmission, with multimedia content comprising a significant portion of this data. Unlike traditional text-based data, Multimedia Big Data (MMBD) presents unique challenges for network infrastructure due to its volume, velocity, and variety. From high-definition video surveillance to real-time medical imaging and industrial monitoring, these applications demand network performance guarantees that extend beyond basic connectivity. As IoT networks evolve to support an ever-increasing number of multimedia-generating devices, the limitations of traditional best-effort service models become increasingly apparent. These models, which treat all data packets equally regardless of their content or time-sensitivity, fail to provide the predictable performance required for many MMBD applications. To address this gap, researchers and industry practitioners have developed various guaranteed service models that aim to provide differentiated treatment for different types of traffic based on their specific requirements.

Building on this foundation, we analyze the mechanisms for flow control and congestion control, which are crucial for maintaining network stability and preventing resource exhaustion. We then examine advanced service models, including Differentiated Services (DiffServ) and Integrated Services (IntServ), highlighting their strengths, weaknesses, and applicability to MMBD-IoT scenarios. Furthermore, we explore specialized techniques such as queuing mechanisms, QoS-aware routing, and call admission control, which play vital roles in implementing effective guaranteed service models.

Through this comprehensive analysis, we aim to provide insights into how network architectures can evolve to better support the demanding requirements of multimedia-rich IoT ecosystems. By understanding the interplay between MMBD characteristics and network service models, we can develop more effective approaches to ensuring satisfactory user experiences in the age of ubiquitous multimedia and connected devices.

2.2 FUNDAMENTALS OF NETWORK ARCHITECTURE

Switched Networks

Switched networks represent the backbone of modern network infrastructure and are particularly relevant for supporting MMBD over IoT. In switched networks, specialized devices (switches and routers) create dedicated communication paths between sending and receiving devices, significantly reducing contention and improving resource utilization compared to shared media networks.

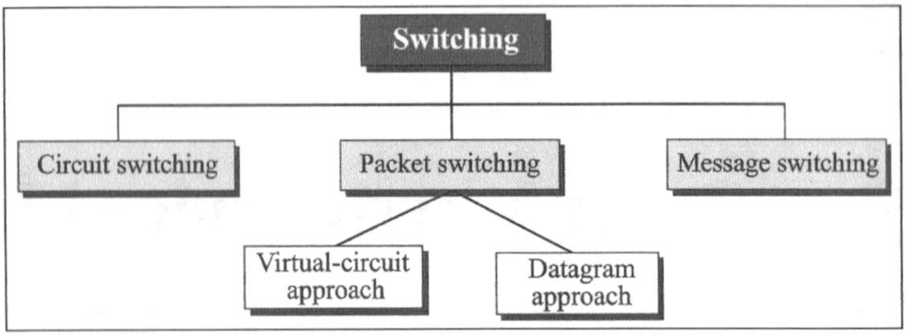

Figure 2.1: *Switched Networks*

Within switched networks, several key switching paradigms exist:

Circuit Switching

This technique establishes a dedicated, end-to-end physical path between communicating parties before data transmission begins. Traditional telephone networks exemplify this approach, where bandwidth is reserved for the duration of the communication. While circuit switching provides strong guarantees for consistent bandwidth and low latency, it suffers from inefficiency when handling bursty data traffic—a common characteristic of many MMBD applications. The reserved resources remain allocated even during periods of inactivity, leading to underutilization of network capacity. Consequently, circuit switching has limited applicability in modern MMBD-IoT contexts, except for specific use cases with predictable and constant bandwidth requirements.

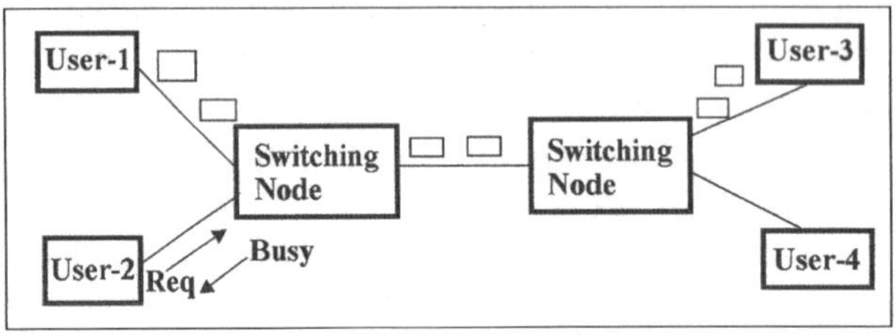

Figure 2.2: *Circuit Switching*

Packet Switching

The dominant paradigm in modern networks, packet switching breaks data into smaller units (packets) that are independently routed through the network. Each packet contains addressing information that allows network devices to forward it toward its destination. The

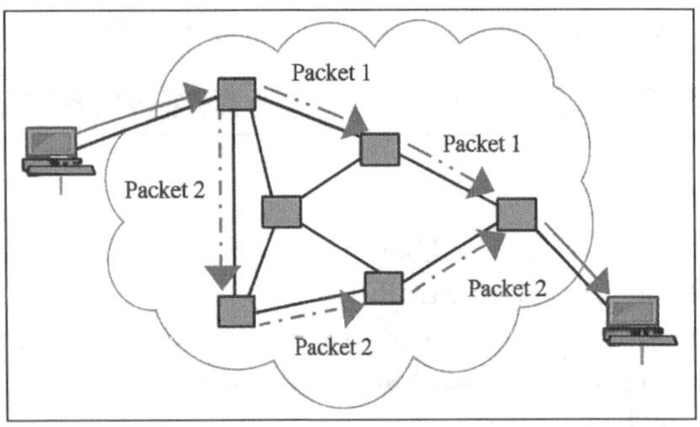

Figure 2.3: *Packet Switching*

Internet Protocol (IP) is fundamentally a packet-switched technology. The key advantage of packet switching is its efficiency in handling bursty traffic and its ability to dynamically allocate network resources based on demand. However, in its basic form, packet switching does not provide inherent guarantees for delivery time or bandwidth, creating challenges for time-sensitive MMBD applications.

Virtual Circuits

This hybrid approach combines elements of both circuit and packet switching. A logical connection (virtual circuit) is established between communicating parties before data transfer begins, and packets follow this predetermined path. Unlike physical circuit switching, virtual circuits do not necessarily reserve bandwidth exclusively along the entire path. This approach offers a middle ground—providing some level of service predictability while maintaining flexibility in resource allocation. Technologies like Multiprotocol Label Switching (MPLS) implement virtual circuit principles to offer enhanced traffic engineering capabilities in IP networks.

Understanding these fundamental switching paradigms is essential for appreciating the constraints and opportunities in implementing guaranteed service models for MMBD over IoT networks.

2.3 SHARED MEDIA NETWORKS

While less prevalent in high-bandwidth MMBD applications, shared media networks still play a role in certain IoT scenarios, particularly in resource-constrained environments. In shared media networks, multiple devices contend for access to a common communication medium, such as a wireless frequency band or a physical cable.

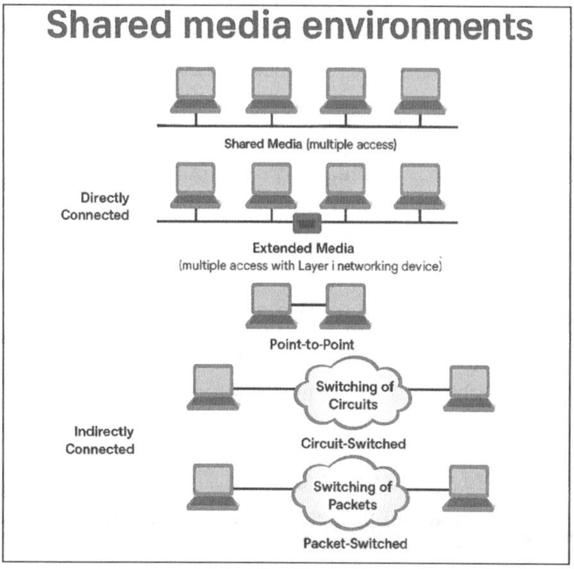

Figure 2.4: *Shared Media Environment*

Traditional Ethernet hubs and early wireless LAN implementations exemplify shared media networks. Communication in these networks typically involves contention-based access methods, where devices follow protocols to determine when they can transmit data.

This approach inherently introduces variability in performance, as the available bandwidth must be divided among all active devices, and collisions can occur when multiple devices attempt to transmit simultaneously.

The contention-based nature of shared media networks presents significant challenges for providing guaranteed service for MMBD applications. As the number of devices increases, so does the likelihood of collisions and performance degradation. This limitation is particularly relevant for IoT deployments that rely on low-power wireless technologies with shared media characteristics.

Despite these challenges, shared media networks remain relevant in certain IoT contexts due to their simplicity, cost-effectiveness, and suitability for low-bandwidth applications. However, for MMBD applications with stringent QoS requirements, switched networks or enhanced shared media technologies with QoS-aware medium access control (MAC) protocols are generally preferred.

2.4 BEST EFFORT SERVICE MODEL AND ITS LIMITATIONS

Characteristics of Best Effort Service

The best effort service model has been the cornerstone of Internet Protocol (IP) networks since their inception. In this model, the network makes its "best effort" to deliver packets to their destination without any guarantees regarding reliability, delay, bandwidth, or other QoS metrics. All packets are treated equally, and forwarding decisions are made based primarily on destination addresses without consideration for the specific requirements of different applications or traffic flows.

The primary advantages of the best effort model lie in its simplicity and scalability. By avoiding the complexity of resource reservation and differentiated treatment, best effort networks can accommodate a large number of users and applications with minimal administrative overhead. This simplicity has been a key factor in the widespread adoption and growth of the Internet.

In best effort networks, end systems are responsible for implementing higher-layer protocols (such as TCP) that provide reliability and flow control on top of the basic delivery service. The network layer focuses solely on forwarding packets toward their destination, leaving issues of congestion control, reliability, and application-specific requirements to be handled by end systems.

Limitations for MMBD-IoT Applications

While the best effort service model has served the Internet well for many applications, it falls short when confronted with the demanding requirements of MMBD over IoT networks. Several key limitations emerge:

1. Unpredictable Delay and Jitter

In a congested best effort network, packets may experience highly variable delays due to queuing at routers and switches. This delay variation, known as jitter, can significantly impact the quality of real-time multimedia applications. For example, in video conferencing or live streaming from IoT sensors, excessive jitter can lead to choppy audio and video, degrading the user experience. Similarly, for time-critical IoT applications such as industrial control systems or healthcare monitoring, unpredictable delays can compromise functionality and safety.

2. Variable Bandwidth Availability

Best effort networks provide no guarantees regarding available bandwidth, which can fluctuate significantly depending on overall network load. During periods of congestion, all traffic flows experience reduced throughput, potentially leading to buffering, quality degradation, or complete interruption of multimedia streams. For IoT devices that must transmit large volumes of multimedia data, such as surveillance cameras or medical imaging devices, inconsistent bandwidth can severely impact their ability to deliver timely and high-quality information.

3. Lack of Packet Loss Guarantees

When network congestion occurs, routers and switches may drop packets to manage buffer overflow. While some applications can tolerate packet loss or recover through retransmission, many MMBD applications are highly sensitive to lost packets. For example, in video streaming, packet loss can result in visible artifacts or frame drops, whereas in critical IoT monitoring applications, lost packets may mean missing vital information. The best effort model provides no mechanisms to protect certain traffic from packet loss during congestion events.

4. Absence of Traffic Prioritization

The equal treatment of all traffic in best effort networks means that delay-sensitive multimedia packets from critical IoT devices receive the same priority as less time-sensitive background transfers. This lack of differentiation makes it impossible to ensure that critical MMBD-IoT applications receive the network resources they need for effective operation, particularly during periods of network congestion.

These limitations clearly demonstrate that the best effort service model is inadequate for supporting the diverse and demanding QoS requirements of MMBD generated and consumed by IoT applications. As IoT deployments increasingly incorporate multimedia capabilities, the need for more sophisticated service models that can provide predictable and differentiated network performance becomes imperative.

2.5 QUALITY OF SERVICE (QoS) METRICS

Essential QoS Parameters

Quality of Service (QoS) metrics provide a framework for quantifying network performance from the perspective of different applications. For MMBD over IoT networks, understanding and measuring these metrics is crucial for implementing effective guaranteed service models. The following QoS parameters are particularly relevant:

1. Bandwidth (Throughput)

This metric refers to the rate at which data can be transferred over a network connection, typically measured in bits per second (bps). For multimedia applications, sufficient bandwidth is essential to support the required data rates for smooth playback or real-time transmission. Different multimedia formats have varying bandwidth requirements—for example, high-definition video requires significantly more bandwidth than audio or still images. In IoT contexts, bandwidth requirements can vary widely depending on the type of sensor data being generated and the frequency of transmission.

2. Delay (Latency)

This parameter measures the time it takes for a data packet to travel from its source to its destination. Delay is composed of several components: propagation delay (time for the signal to travel through the physical medium), transmission delay (time to place the packet on the link), queuing delay (time spent waiting in buffers), and processing delay (time for routers to process the packet header). For interactive multimedia applications, such as video conferencing or remote control of IoT devices, low delay is crucial for ensuring a responsive user experience. Different applications have different delay tolerance thresholds—for example, voice communication typically requires end-to-end delay below 150ms for acceptable quality, while some industrial control applications may require even lower delays.

3. Jitter (Delay Variation)

Jitter refers to the variation in delay experienced by packets within the same data stream. High jitter can be particularly problematic for real-time multimedia applications, as it can lead to uneven playback and degraded quality. To mitigate jitter, receivers typically implement jitter buffers that temporarily store incoming packets to smooth out timing variations. However, these buffers introduce additional delay, creating a trade-off between jitter reduction and overall latency. For MMBD-IoT applications like live video surveillance or remote monitoring, minimizing jitter is essential for maintaining the integrity and usefulness of the transmitted content.

4. Packet Loss Rate

This metric indicates the percentage of packets that fail to reach their destination. Packet loss can occur due to various factors, including network congestion, buffer overflows, or physical transmission errors. Different multimedia applications have varying tolerance for packet loss—for example, file transfers require zero loss (though they can recover through retransmission), while real-time video may tolerate some loss depending on the encoding scheme and error concealment techniques employed. In IoT scenarios, the acceptable packet loss rate depends on the criticality of the application; sensor readings for non-critical monitoring might tolerate some loss, while control commands for critical systems might require near-perfect reliability.

5. Reliability

This encompassing metric refers to the overall dependability of the network in delivering data correctly and consistently. It includes aspects such as packet loss, error rates, and network availability. For MMBD-IoT applications, reliability is particularly important in critical domains such as healthcare, industrial automation, or public safety, where the consequences of data loss or corruption can be severe.

Application-Specific QoS Requirements

The QoS requirements of MMBD-IoT applications vary significantly based on their specific characteristics and purposes. Understanding these requirements is essential for designing appropriate guaranteed service models. Some common MMBD-IoT application categories and their typical QoS needs include:

- **Real-time Video Surveillance:** IoT cameras used for security and monitoring typically require moderate to high bandwidth (depending on resolution and frame rate), low delay (especially for PTZ control), low jitter, and moderate packet loss tolerance (depending on the encoding scheme).

- **Remote Healthcare Monitoring:** Medical devices transmitting vital signs or diagnostic images may require guaranteed bandwidth, low delay for real time monitoring, very low packet loss for critical data, and high reliability.
- **Industrial Automation and Control:** IoT sensors and actuators in industrial settings often require low bandwidth but extremely low delay and jitter, minimal packet loss, and very high reliability, particularly for closed-loop control systems.
- **Smart Home Entertainment:** IoT devices for home entertainment (e.g., streaming devices, smart TVs) typically require high bandwidth, moderate delay tolerance, low jitter, and moderate packet loss tolerance with appropriate error concealment.
- **Environmental Monitoring:** Distributed IoT sensors for environmental monitoring may have lower bandwidth requirements but need reliability and predictable delivery for aggregated data analysis.

These diverse requirements highlight the need for flexible and adaptable guaranteed service models that can accommodate the specific QoS needs of different MMBD-IoT applications, ensuring optimal performance across a wide range of scenarios.

2.6 FLOW CONTROL AND CONGESTION CONTROL

Flow Control Mechanisms

Flow control is a critical mechanism in data networks that prevents a sender from overwhelming a receiver with more data than it can process. In MMBD-IoT contexts, where devices might have varying processing capabilities and buffer sizes, effective flow control is essential for preventing data loss and ensuring smooth operation.

The primary aim of flow control is to regulate the rate at which a sender transmits data based on the receiver's processing capacity. This is typically implemented at the transport layer (e.g., TCP) or link layer of the network stack.

Several key flow control mechanisms include:

1. Window-Based Flow Control

This widely used approach involves the receiver advertising a "window" that indicates how much data it is willing to accept. The sender can then transmit up to this amount of data before requiring acknowledgment. As the receiver processes data, it advances the window, allowing the sender to transmit more.

TCP's flow control mechanism is a classic example of window-based flow control, where the receiver advertises it receive window size in every acknowledgment packet. In MMBD-IoT scenarios, this approach helps prevent powerful data sources (e.g., video cameras) from overwhelming resource-constrained receivers.

Rate-Based Flow Control: Instead of using a window mechanism, rate-based flow control directly regulates the rate at which data is transmitted. The receiver provides feedback about its capacity, and the sender adjusts its transmission rate accordingly. This approach is particularly useful for streaming multimedia applications where a constant or adjustable bit rate is desired. Protocols like the Real-time Transport Protocol (RTP) and Real-time Transport Control Protocol (RTCP) incorporate rate-based flow control mechanisms that are well-suited for MMBD applications.

2. Credit-Based Flow Control

In this approach, the receiver issues "credits" to the sender, indicating how much data it can accept. The sender can only transmit data if it has sufficient credits, and credits are replenished as the receiver processes data. This mechanism provides fine-grained control over data flow and is particularly useful in environments with limited buffer space, such as resource-constrained IoT devices.

Effective flow control is essential for preventing buffer overflow at receivers, which can lead to packet loss and degraded performance. In MMBD-IoT scenarios, where devices with varying capabilities must interact, adaptive flow control mechanisms that can adjust to the characteristics of different devices are particularly valuable.

Congestion Control Strategies

While flow control focuses on protecting the receiver, congestion control aims to prevent network overload by regulating traffic when the aggregate demand exceeds available capacity. Congestion occurs when too many packets are present in the network, leading to increased delays, packet loss, and reduced throughput for all users. Effective congestion control is particularly important for MMBD-IoT networks, where the massive volume of multimedia data can easily overwhelm network resources.

Several congestion control strategies are commonly employed:

1. TCP Congestion Control

The Transmission Control Protocol (TCP) incorporates sophisticated congestion control algorithms that adjust the sender's transmission rate based on network conditions. These algorithms include: - Slow Start: Initially increasing the transmission rate exponentially until detecting congestion - Congestion Avoidance: Gradually increasing the rate after congestion is detected - Fast Retransmit and Fast Recovery: Quickly recovering from packet loss without drastic rate reduction

While TCP's congestion control is effective for many applications, it may not be optimal for all MMBD scenarios, particularly those with real-time requirements that cannot tolerate the delays associated with retransmissions.

2. Active Queue Management (AQM

These techniques aim to prevent congestion before it becomes severe by actively managing router queues. Examples include: - Random Early Detection (RED): Probabilistically dropping packets as queue length increases - Explicit Congestion Notification (ECN): Marking packets to signal impending congestion without dropping them - Controlled Delay (CoDel): Managing queue delays to prevent bufferbloat.

AQM techniques can significantly improve network performance during congestion events, benefiting MMBD-IoT applications that are sensitive to delay and packet loss.

3. QoS-Based Congestion Control

This approach involves differentiated treatment of traffic during congestion based on QoS requirements. By prioritizing critical MMBD-IoT traffic during congestion events, the network can ensure that high-priority applications continue to receive adequate resources even when the network is overloaded.

4. Cross-Layer Congestion Control

These techniques leverage information from multiple layers of the network stack to make more informed congestion control decisions. For example, application-layer information about video frame importance can be used to make smarter decisions about which packets to drop during congestion. This approach is particularly valuable for MMBD applications, where the impact of packet loss can vary significantly depending on the content of the packets.

Effective congestion control is essential for maintaining network stability and ensuring fair resource allocation, particularly in MMBD-IoT environments where traffic patterns can be highly variable and resource demands can change rapidly. By implementing appropriate congestion control strategies, networks can provide more predictable performance for MMBD applications even under challenging conditions.

2.7 DIFFERENTIATED SERVICES (DIFFSERV) ARCHITECTURE

DiffServ Principles and Components

The Differentiated Services (DiffServ) architecture represents a scalable approach to providing QoS in IP networks. Unlike more complex resource reservation schemes, DiffServ focuses on traffic classification and per-hop behaviors to deliver differentiated treatment to different traffic classes. This approach offers a more practical solution for managing QoS across large networks, making it particularly relevant for MMBD-IoT environments with diverse traffic types and requirements.

The DiffServ architecture is built around several key components:

1. Traffic Classification and Marking

At the edge of the DiffServ domain (typically the first router an IoT device connects to), traffic is classified into different service classes based on various criteria such as application type, source/destination addresses, or port numbers. Each packet is then marked with a Differentiated Services Code Point (DSCP) value in the IP header's Type of Service (ToS) field. This marking determines how the packet will be treated as it traverses the network. For MMBD-IoT applications, classification might be based on the type of multimedia content (e.g., real-time video vs. background file transfer) or the criticality of the application (e.g., healthcare monitoring vs. entertainment).

2. Per-Hop Behavior (PHB)

Within the DiffServ domain, each router implements specific Per-Hop Behaviors (PHBs) for each DSCP value. A PHB defines how packets with a particular DSCP marking should be treated as they traverse the router. This treatment can include aspects such as: - Queuing priority: Determining which packets get serviced first - Scheduling algorithms: Allocating bandwidth among different traffic classes - Drop precedence: Determining which packets are dropped first during congestion

3. Behavior Aggregates (BAs

Traffic with the same DSCP value that traverses a particular network node is treated according to the same PHB, forming a behavior aggregate. This aggregate treatment is what allows DiffServ to be more scalable than per-flow resource reservation schemes, as routers maintain state for a limited number of traffic classes rather than for individual flows.

4. Traffic Conditioning

To ensure that traffic entering the DiffServ domain conforms to service level agreements (SLAs), traffic conditioning mechanisms may be applied at the network edge. These mechanisms include:

- **Metering:** Measuring the rate at which traffic enters the network
- **Policing:** Dropping or remarking packets that exceed specified rate limits
- **Shaping:** Delaying packets to ensure they conform to a specified traffic profile

DiffServ PHB Classes

DiffServ defines several standardized PHB classes, each designed to address specific QoS requirements:

1. Default PHB (Best Effort

This is the default treatment for traffic that is not classified into any other PHB class. It provides the same service as traditional best effort networks, with no specific guarantees. In MMBD-IoT contexts, this might be appropriate for non-critical background transfers or for traffic when the network is underutilized.

2. Expedited Forwarding (EF) PHB

The EF PHB is designed to provide low-latency, low-jitter, and assured bandwidth service. It is implemented by ensuring that the EF traffic departure rate from any node is at least as fast as its arrival rate, effectively minimizing queuing delay. This PHB is particularly well-suited for delay-sensitive MMBD-IoT applications such as real-time video conferencing, voice over IP, or critical control signals in industrial IoT.

3. Assured Forwarding (AF) PHB Group

The AF PHB group provides different levels of forwarding assurance for IP packets. It defines four AF classes, each with three drop precedence levels, resulting in twelve distinct DSCP values. The four classes represent different levels of resource allocation (primarily bandwidth), while the drop precedence levels determine the relative importance of packets within each class during congestion. For MMBD-IoT applications, the AF PHB group allows for nuanced service differentiation—for example, different types of video streams could be assigned to different AF classes based on their importance, with I-frames given lower drop precedence than P-frames within each class.

4. Class Selector (CS) PHBs

These PHBs provide backward compatibility with the IP Precedence field in the original IP ToS byte. They define eight priority levels, with higher values indicating higher priority. CS PHBs can be useful for simple prioritization schemes in MMBD-IoT networks, particularly when integrating with legacy systems.

The DiffServ architecture provides a flexible framework for implementing QoS in MMBD-IoT networks. By appropriately classifying and marking traffic, and by configuring PHBs to align with application requirements, network operators can provide differentiated service levels that support the diverse QoS needs of multimedia applications. However, effective implementation requires careful planning and configuration to ensure that the desired PHBs are consistently applied across the DiffServ domain.

2.8 INTEGRATED SERVICES (INTSERV) ARCHITECTURE

IntServ Principles and Components

The Integrated Services (IntServ) architecture represents a more rigorous approach to QoS than DiffServ, focusing on per-flow resource reservation to provide strong guarantees for individual traffic flows. While more complex to implement at scale, IntServ offers the potential for more precise QoS control, which can be valuable for certain high-priority MMBD-IoT applications. The IntServ architecture is built around several key components:

1. **Flow Specification:** IntServ requires applications to specify their traffic characteristics and QoS requirements through a flow specification (flowspec). This typically includes parameters such as:
    - **Traffic specification (Tspec):** Describing the traffic profile (e.g., peak rate, burst size)
    - **Request specification (Rspec):** Specifying the desired QoS (e.g., bandwidth, delay bounds)
    - For MMBD-IoT applications, the flowspec would capture the specific characteristics of the multimedia stream, such as the video bitrate, frame rate, and acceptable delay bounds.
2. **Resource Reservation Protocol (RSVP):** RSVP is the signaling protocol most commonly associated with IntServ. It allows applications to request specific QoS levels from the network and enables routers along the path to reserve the necessary resources. The RSVP process involves:
    - **Path messages:** Sent from the sender to the receiver, establishing the path and collecting information about available resources
    - **Resv messages:** Sent from the receiver back to the sender, requesting specific resources along the established path
    - **Reservation state:** Maintained at each router along the path for the duration of the flow
3. **Admission Control:** This component is responsible for determining whether a new reservation request can be accommodated without violating existing guarantees. Each router along the path performs admission control based on its available resources and the requested QoS. If any router along the path cannot accommodate the request, the reservation is rejected. This ensures that QoS guarantees are only made when they can be reliably delivered.
4. **Packet Classifier and Scheduler:** Once a reservation is established, routers implement packet classification to identify packets belonging to specific flows and scheduling mechanisms to ensure that the reserved resources are provided to those flows. This may involve sophisticated queue management and scheduling algorithms to meet the guaranteed service levels.

IntServ Service Classes

IntServ defines several service classes to address different QoS requirements:

1. **Guaranteed Service:** This service class provides strict mathematical bounds on end-to-end queuing delay, essentially guaranteeing that packets will arrive within a

specified time constraint. It is designed for applications that require hard real-time guarantees, such as certain types of industrial control systems or critical medical applications in IoT contexts. Guaranteed Service requires resource reservation and admission control at each network node along the path.

2. **Controlled Load Service:** This service class aims to provide a quality of service similar to that of an unloaded network, even during periods of congestion. While it does not provide the strict mathematical guarantees of Guaranteed Service, it ensures that the vast majority of packets will experience little or no queuing delay. Controlled Load Service is suitable for adaptive real-time applications, such as many multimedia streaming applications in IoT environments, which can tolerate occasional QoS variations.
3. **Best Effort Service:** This is the default service class for traffic that does not request specific QoS guarantees. It provides the same service as traditional best effort networks, with no specific guarantees regarding bandwidth, delay, or packet loss.

IntServ Limitations and Applicability

While IntServ offers strong QoS guarantees, it faces several challenges that limit its widespread deployment, particularly in large-scale MMBD-IoT environments:

1. **Scalability Concerns:** Maintaining per-flow state at each router along the path can be resource-intensive, especially in core networks handling thousands or millions of flows. This limits the scalability of pure IntServ implementations.
2. **Signaling Overhead:** The RSVP signaling protocol introduces additional overhead, both in terms of bandwidth consumption and processing requirements. This overhead can be particularly problematic in resource-constrained IoT networks.
3. **End-to-End Deployment Requirement:** Achieving the full benefits of IntServ requires support for RSVP and resource reservation throughout the end-to-end path. This can be challenging in heterogeneous networks that may include segments without IntServ support.

Despite these limitations, IntServ principles remain valuable for specific MMBD-IoT scenarios where strong QoS guarantees are essential, such as:

- Critical industrial control systems requiring deterministic performance
- Medical applications with strict real-time requirements
- High-value multimedia applications in controlled network environments

In practice, hybrid approaches that combine elements of IntServ (typically at the network edge) with more scalable DiffServ techniques (in the network core) may offer a pragmatic solution for providing effective QoS guarantees in MMBD-IoT environments.

2.9 QUEUING TECHNIQUES FOR QUALITY OF SERVICE

Basic Queuing Disciplines

Queuing techniques are fundamental mechanisms employed in network devices to manage traffic and implement QoS policies. When multiple packets compete for limited bandwidth, queuing disciplines determine the order in which packets are processed and transmitted, directly impacting metrics such as delay, jitter, and loss. For MMBD-IoT applications with diverse QoS requirements, appropriate queuing techniques are essential for ensuring satisfactory performance.

Several basic queuing disciplines form the foundation of QoS implementation:

1. First-In, First-Out (FIFO)

The simplest queuing discipline, FIFO processes packets strictly in the order they arrive. While straightforward to implement, FIFO offers no differentiation between traffic types and can lead to head-of-line blocking, where high-priority packets are delayed behind lower-priority ones. In MMBD-IoT contexts, FIFO is generally insufficient for providing guaranteed service, as it cannot prioritize time-sensitive multimedia traffic over less critical data.

2. Priority Queuing (PQ)

This discipline categorizes packets into multiple priority levels, with higher-priority queues always served before lower-priority ones. PQ ensures that high-priority traffic experiences minimal delay, making it well-suited for time-sensitive MMBD applications. However, strict priority queuing can lead to starvation of lower-priority traffic during periods of heavy high-priority load.

In MMBD-IoT scenarios, PQ might be appropriate for critical control traffic or real-time video streams that require immediate forwarding, but safeguards are needed to prevent complete starvation of other traffic classes.

3. Round Robin (RR)

This discipline serves queues in a cyclic fashion, giving each queue an opportunity to send packets before moving to the next queue. Standard RR allocates equal service time to each queue regardless of packet size, which can lead to unfair bandwidth allocation. In MMBD-IoT networks, simple RR might be used for traffic classes with similar priority levels but would not provide the differentiation needed for diverse multimedia applications.

Advanced Queuing Techniques

Building on basic queuing disciplines, several advanced techniques offer more sophisticated control over traffic handling:

1. Weighted Fair Queuing (WFQ)

WFQ allocates bandwidth among different traffic flows based on assigned weights, aiming to provide fair service without complete starvation of any flow. It approximates the theoretical Generalized Processor Sharing (GPS) model, which allows each flow to receive a weighted share of the available bandwidth.

WFQ is particularly valuable for MMBD-IoT environments with diverse traffic types, as it allows network administrators to allocate bandwidth proportionally to the importance or requirements of different applications.

2. Class-Based Weighted Fair Queuing (CBWFQ)

This extension of WFQ groups traffic into classes based on various criteria (e.g., protocol, application type) and applies weighted fair queuing to these classes rather than individual flows. CBWFQ provides better scalability than per-flow WFQ while still offering differentiated service. In MMBD-IoT contexts, CBWFQ could be used to allocate specific bandwidth guarantees to different categories of multimedia traffic (e.g., video surveillance, environmental sensors, voice communication).

3. Low Latency Queuing (LLQ)

LLQ combines strict priority queuing for delay-sensitive traffic with CBWFQ for other traffic classes. This hybrid approach ensures that real-time traffic (e.g., voice, video) receives immediate service while still providing fair treatment to other traffic classes. LLQ is particularly well-suited for MMBD-IoT environments where some applications have strict delay requirements while others primarily need bandwidth guarantees.

4. Random Early Detection (RED)

RED is a congestion avoidance mechanism that proactively drops packets before queue buffers become completely full. By monitoring the average queue size and dropping packets probabilistically when it exceeds certain thresholds, RED helps prevent synchronized packet drops and global synchronization issues. Weighted RED (WRED) extends this concept by applying different drop probabilities to different traffic classes, providing another layer of service differentiation. In MMBD-IoT networks, RED and WRED can help maintain stable performance during periods of congestion, reducing the impact on multimedia quality.

5. Deficit Round Robin (DRR)

This enhancement to the basic round robin discipline addresses the fairness issues related to variable packet sizes. DRR assigns a quantum of service to each queue and keeps track of deficits when a queue cannot send a packet due to size constraints. This approach ensures fair bandwidth allocation regardless of packet size variations, which is particularly relevant for MMBD traffic with variable packet sizes.

The selection and configuration of queuing techniques should be tailored to the specific requirements of the MMBD-IoT environment. By implementing appropriate queuing disciplines at network devices, operators can significantly improve the quality of service for multimedia applications, ensuring that critical traffic receives the necessary resources while maintaining fair treatment for all traffic classes.

2.10 QoS-AWARE ROUTING

Traditional routing protocols primarily focus on finding the shortest or most efficient path between a source and a destination based on metrics like hop count or link bandwidth. However, in networks carrying MMBD with diverse QoS requirements, simply finding a path is not enough; the chosen path must also be capable of supporting the specific QoS needs of the traffic flow. QoS-aware routing aims to address this by incorporating QoS considerations into the path selection process.

Principles of QoS-Aware Routing

- **QoS Metrics in Routing Decisions**: QoS-aware routing protocols consider metrics like available bandwidth, delay, jitter, packet loss probability, and link reliability when selecting a path.
- **Path Selection Based on QoS Requirements**: When a new traffic flow with specific QoS requirements (e.g., minimum bandwidth, maximum delay) needs to be routed, the QoS-aware routing protocol attempts to find a path that can satisfy these constraints.
- **Resource Availability Information**: Routers need to have information about the current availability of network resources (e.g., link bandwidth, buffer space) along different paths to make informed routing decisions. This information might be

obtained through extensions to existing routing protocols or through separate resource management protocols.

QoS-Aware Routing Algorithms

Several algorithms have been developed to address QoS-aware routing challenges:

1. **Constraint-Based Routing (CBR)**: This approach applies constraints to the path selection process based on QoS requirements. Paths that do not meet the constraints are pruned from consideration, and the routing decision is made from the remaining feasible paths.
2. **Multi-Constraint Path Selection**: When multiple QoS constraints need to be satisfied simultaneously (e.g., both bandwidth and delay requirements), more complex algorithms are needed. This is an NP-complete problem, but several heuristic approaches provide practical solutions.
3. **QoS Extensions to Existing Protocols**: Rather than developing entirely new protocols, QoS extensions have been added to existing routing protocols like OSPF (Open Shortest Path First) and BGP (Border Gateway Protocol).

QoS Routing Metrics

The effectiveness of QoS-aware routing depends on the metrics used to evaluate potential paths:

- **Bandwidth**: The available bandwidth along a path is a crucial metric for multimedia applications requiring high data rates.
- **Delay**: End-to-end delay is critical for real-time applications. This includes transmission delay, propagation delay, queuing delay, and processing delay.
- **Jitter**: Variation in packet arrival times affects the quality of real-time applications. Low jitter is essential for voice and video applications.
- **Packet Loss**: The probability of packet loss along a path affects the reliability of data transmission.
- **Energy Efficiency**: In IoT networks, the energy consumption of routing paths becomes an important consideration for battery-powered devices.

Implementation Approaches

QoS-aware routing can be implemented using various approaches:

1. **Source Routing**: The source node computes the entire path based on QoS requirements and includes this information in the packet header.
2. **Distributed Routing**: Each node along the path makes local decisions based on QoS information.
3. **Hierarchical Routing**: QoS-aware routing decisions are made at different levels of the network hierarchy, with aggregated QoS information used at higher levels.
4. **SDN-Based Approaches**: Software-Defined Networking (SDN) enables centralized control of routing decisions, allowing for more sophisticated QoS-aware routing strategies.

Challenges in QoS-Aware Routing for MMBD-IoT

- **Complexity**: Incorporating QoS metrics into routing algorithms and protocols adds significant complexity.

- **Scalability**: Maintaining and disseminating real-time information about resource availability across a large and dynamic MMBD-IoT network can be challenging.
- **Dynamic Network Conditions**: The QoS characteristics of network links (e.g., available bandwidth) can change rapidly due to varying traffic loads, making it difficult to guarantee that a chosen path will continue to meet the QoS requirements throughout the duration of a flow.
- **Trade-offs**: Selecting a path that meets the QoS requirements of one flow might lead to suboptimal paths for other flows.
- **Computational Overhead**: QoS-aware routing algorithms generally require more computational resources than traditional routing algorithms.

QoS-Aware Routing in Wireless and Mobile Networks

In wireless and mobile MMBD-IoT environments, QoS-aware routing faces additional challenges:

- **Link Instability**: Wireless links are inherently less stable than wired links, making QoS guarantees more difficult.
- **Mobility**: Device mobility can lead to frequent path changes, requiring dynamic adaptation of QoS-aware routes.
- **Resource Constraints**: Many wireless IoT devices have limited energy, processing power, and memory, constraining the complexity of routing algorithms.
- **Interference**: Wireless interference can significantly impact link quality and available bandwidth, requiring consideration in QoS-aware routing decisions.

Future Directions

Research in QoS-aware routing for MMBD-IoT is progressing in several directions:

- **Machine Learning Approaches**: Using ML algorithms to predict network conditions and optimize QoS-aware routing decisions.
- **Intent-Based Networking**: Allowing applications to specify their QoS intent rather than specific technical requirements, with the network handling the translation to appropriate routing decisions.
- **Cross-Layer Optimization**: Integrating QoS-aware routing with other layers of the network stack for more holistic optimization.
- **Edge Computing Integration**: Considering the placement of compute resources in edge locations as part of QoS-aware routing decisions.

Despite these challenges, QoS-aware routing is a crucial aspect of providing guaranteed service for demanding MMBD-IoT applications. Research efforts are ongoing to develop more efficient and scalable QoS-aware routing protocols that can adapt to the dynamic nature of modern networks. In scenarios where certain MMBD flows have critical QoS needs (e.g., real-time control data in industrial IoT), deploying QoS-aware routing mechanisms can significantly enhance the reliability and performance of the system.

2.11 CALL ADMISSION CONTROL

Call Admission Control (CAC) is a mechanism used in networks that provide QoS guarantees to decide whether to accept a new connection or flow based on the availability of sufficient resources to meet its QoS requirements without violating the guarantees already provided to existing flows. CAC is particularly relevant in scenarios where network resources are limited, such as in wireless networks or in Intserv-based architectures with explicit resource reservations.

How Call Admission Control Works

1. **QoS Requirement Specification**: When a new application or IoT device wants to initiate a communication flow that requires guaranteed QoS (e.g., a specific bandwidth or delay bound), it first specifies its QoS requirements to the network.
2. **Resource Availability Check**: The network (typically a network node like a router or a central controller) checks if it has enough available resources along the intended path to satisfy the QoS requirements of the new flow. This check considers the resources currently being used by existing flows and the total capacity of the network links.
3. **Admission Decision**: Based on the resource availability check, the network makes an admission decision:
    - **Accept**: If sufficient resources are available, the network accepts the new flow, allocates the necessary resources, and allows the communication to proceed with the requested QoS guarantees.
    - **Reject**: If sufficient resources are not available, the network rejects the new flow to protect the QoS guarantees of the existing flows.
    - **Negotiate**: In some advanced CAC implementations, if the original QoS requirements cannot be met, the network might negotiate with the application to accept a lower level of QoS that can be provided with the available resources.
4. **Resource Reservation**: Once a flow is accepted, the network reserves the necessary resources (e.g., bandwidth, buffer space) for that flow along its path. These reservations ensure that the flow will have access to the promised resources throughout its duration.

Benefits of Call Admission Control in MMBD-IoT

- **Protection of Existing Flows**: By rejecting new flows when resources are insufficient, CAC ensures that existing flows with QoS guarantees are not negatively impacted by network congestion.
- **Predictable Performance**: Applications and IoT devices can rely on receiving the QoS they were promised, leading to more predictable and consistent performance.
- **Efficient Resource Utilization**: CAC helps in better utilization of network resources by preventing oversubscription and the resulting degradation in service quality.
- **Prioritization**: In multi-class networks, CAC can prioritize high-priority traffic by reserving resources for critical applications, ensuring they receive the required QoS even during network congestion.

Challenges in Implementing CAC for MMBD-IoT

- **Distributed Decision Making**: In large-scale MMBD-IoT networks, making admission decisions in a distributed manner while ensuring consistency across the network can be challenging.

- **Dynamic Traffic Patterns**: IoT traffic can be highly variable and bursty, making it difficult to accurately estimate resource requirements for new flows.
- **Overhead**: The signaling and processing overhead associated with CAC mechanisms can be significant, especially in resource-constrained IoT environments.
- **Integration with Existing Protocols**: Integrating CAC with existing network protocols and architectures requires careful design to ensure compatibility and efficiency.

2.12 TRAFFIC ENGINEERING AND LOAD BALANCING

Traffic Engineering (TE) and Load Balancing are complementary approaches to optimizing network performance and resource utilization in MMBD-IoT networks. While traditional routing protocols focus on finding the shortest or most efficient path between endpoints, TE and load balancing take a more holistic view of network resources to distribute traffic efficiently across multiple paths.

Principles of Traffic Engineering

- **Global Resource Optimization**: TE aims to optimize the overall utilization of network resources rather than focusing on individual flows or paths.
- **Path Diversity Exploitation**: TE leverages the availability of multiple paths between source and destination to distribute traffic efficiently.
- **Congestion Avoidance**: By redistributing traffic away from congested links or nodes, TE helps prevent bottlenecks and ensures more consistent performance.
- **QoS-Aware Traffic Distribution**: Advanced TE techniques consider the QoS requirements of different traffic classes when making traffic distribution decisions.

Load Balancing Techniques for MMBD-IoT

- **Equal-Cost Multi-Path (ECMP)**: Distributes traffic evenly across multiple paths of equal cost, typically using hash-based mechanisms to ensure that packets belonging to the same flow follow the same path.
- **Weighted Load Balancing**: Assigns different weights to different paths based on their capacity, current load, or other metrics, distributing traffic proportionally to these weights.
- **Dynamic Load Balancing**: Continuously monitors network conditions and adapts the traffic distribution in real-time to respond to changes in traffic patterns or network state.
- **Application-Aware Load Balancing**: Considers the specific requirements of different applications or IoT devices when making load balancing decisions, ensuring that traffic is directed to paths that can best support its QoS needs.

Benefits of TE and Load Balancing in MMBD-IoT

- **Improved Resource Utilization**: By distributing traffic across multiple paths, TE and load balancing help in achieving more efficient utilization of network resources.

- **Enhanced Reliability**: Traffic can be rerouted around failed or congested links, improving the overall reliability of the network.
- **Scalability**: TE and load balancing techniques can help networks scale more effectively by preventing individual links or nodes from becoming bottlenecks.
- **Better QoS Support**: By avoiding congestion and optimizing resource allocation, TE and load balancing contribute to better QoS support for demanding MMBD-IoT applications.

Challenges in Implementing TE and Load Balancing

- **Complexity**: Implementing sophisticated TE and load balancing mechanisms can add significant complexity to network management and operations.
- **Overhead**: The monitoring and control overhead associated with dynamic TE and load balancing can be substantial.
- **Interaction with Other Mechanisms**: TE and load balancing need to work in harmony with other QoS mechanisms such as QoS-aware routing and CAC to ensure consistent and predictable performance.
- **Balancing Stability and Responsiveness**: TE and load balancing algorithms need to find the right balance between stability (avoiding frequent changes that could disrupt traffic) and responsiveness to changing network conditions.

In MMBD-IoT environments, where traffic patterns are diverse and dynamic, effective TE and load balancing are essential for maintaining high network performance and ensuring that critical applications receive the necessary QoS. As MMBD-IoT networks continue to evolve, we can expect to see more sophisticated and automated TE and load balancing techniques that leverage artificial intelligence and machine learning to optimize network performance in real-time.

2.13 MULTICAST ROUTING AND PROTOCOL INDEPENDENT MULTICAST (PIM)

Multicast routing is a network method that has been developed to effectively send data from one or more sources to many receivers without duplication. Multicast differs from unicast, which sends independent copies of data to each recipient, in that multicast sends data once and copies it within the network as necessary, maximizing bandwidth and minimizing congestion in the network.

This method is especially useful for use in applications like live video streaming, online gaming, stock market news, and collaborative conferencing, where data needs to be distributed to many users at the same time. To facilitate multicast communication, routers employ multicast routing protocols to dynamically control group membership and effectively forward multicast packets.

One of the most popular multicast routing protocols is Protocol Independent Multicast (PIM), which works independently of a particular unicast routing protocol. PIM is not based on a specific routing table but makes use of the available unicast routing infrastructure to construct and manage multicast distribution trees. PIM is adaptive and can be configured to work in various modes for different network topologies and traffic patterns. The two principal versions of PIM are PIM Sparse Mode (PIM-SM) and PIM Dense Mode (PIM-DM).

PIM Sparse Mode (PIM-SM) is suited for networks in which multicast receivers are spread thinly, so that only a few network segments need multicast traffic. In order to maximize efficiency, PIM-SM constructs multicast distribution trees with the aid of a Rendezvous Point (RP), which serves as a meeting point for senders and receivers. Rather than inundating the network with multicast traffic, PIM-SM creates on-demand paths, or Shared Trees and Shortest Path Trees (SPT), only when receivers join a multicast group explicitly. This method saves bandwidth and avoids unnecessary data transmission in regions without interested receivers.

PIM Dense Mode (PIM-DM), on the other hand, is appropriate for networks where multicast receivers are densely distributed throughout the network. As compared to PIM-SM, PIM-DM first floods multicast traffic on all network segments and subsequently trims unnecessary branches where no receivers are found. This "flood-and-prune" feature makes multicast data available to all possible recipients but can cause redundant bandwidth usage in networks where receivers are not evenly distributed. Owing to this aggressive flooding, PIM-DM is more appropriate for small, well-populated networks having a high number of multicast receivers.

Both PIM-SM and PIM-DM have respective strengths based on network topology and multicast traffic spread. Although PIM-SM is the favored choice for wide-area, internet-scale multicast operations because of its receiver-driven, efficient design, PIM-DM performs better in smaller networks where multicast traffic is dispersed. Both these variations of the protocol support scalable, efficient multicast communication, allowing data to be distributed only where required while minimizing utilization of network resources.

SUMMARY

Media networks that are shared, integrated, and switched form the basis of modern communiction systems with the use of circuit switching, packet switching, and virtual circuits for data transfer. Smooth handoffs require flow and congestion control methods to mitigate data loss as well as facilitate traffic smoothness. The Best Effort Service Model is widely accepted but it is not good at ensuring reilable data delivery, thus leading to the requirement of implementing Quality of Service (QoS) metrics. Networks offered to the public DiffServ and IntServ are providing better Queuing Intergace Traffic Control by Weighted Fair Queuing (WFQ) and its variants and Random Early Detection (RED) methods for congestion avoidance. Efficient resource pre-allocation is guaranteed by Policing and traffic shaping delay sensitive data packets to ensure the required level of quality in the network. Activities such as multicasting with the help of Internet Group Management Protocol (IGMP) and Sparse Mode Protocol Independent Multicast (PIM) along with Dense Mode PIM (PIM DM) enable efficient usage of the allocated bandwidth by optimizing multicast data delivery. These technologies together work towards enhancing an integrated network's performance, reliability, and scalability in an environment of high demand for communication services.

3

UNIT

Multimedia Transport

3.1 INTRODUCTION TO MULTIMEDIA TRANSPORT IN IoT

The Internet of Things (IoT) has revolutionized the way we interact with technology, creating a vast network of interconnected devices that continuously generate, process, and exchange data. A significant portion of this data consists of multimedia content—images, audio, and video—collectively referred to as Multimedia Big Data (MMBD). The sheer volume, velocity, and variety of this multimedia data present unique challenges for its efficient and reliable transport across networks.

Multimedia transport in the IoT context refers to the processes and technologies involved in moving multimedia data from its point of generation (typically IoT sensors and devices) to its point of consumption (end-users, analytics platforms, or automated decision-making systems). Unlike traditional data transport, multimedia transport must contend with the large file sizes, real-time requirements, and heterogeneous nature of multimedia content.

The proliferation of multimedia-enabled IoT devices has created unprecedented demands on network infrastructure. From security cameras streaming high-definition video to wearable health monitors capturing and transmitting physiological data, these devices generate massive amounts of multimedia content that must be efficiently transported across diverse network environments with varying capabilities and constraints.

As we delve deeper into this topic, we will explore various aspects of multimedia transport, including transport protocols, streaming technologies, quality of experience considerations, and emerging trends that are shaping the future of this field. Our goal is to provide a comprehensive resource that bridges theoretical concepts with practical implementations, equipping readers with the knowledge needed to address the complex challenges of multimedia transport in the ever-expanding realm of IoT.

End-to-End Solutions for Multimedia Big Data

Multimedia transport in IoT environments requires a holistic, end-to-end perspective that considers each phase of the data lifecycle. This chapter examines the journey of multimedia data from its origin to its eventual use, highlighting the interconnections between transport mechanisms and other aspects of the MMBD lifecycle.

Multimedia Data Lifecycle

The lifecycle of multimedia data in IoT applications typically encompasses several key stages:

- **Data Acquisition:** At this initial stage, IoT devices equipped with cameras, microphones, and other sensors capture multimedia data. The characteristics of this data—resolution, frame rate, bit depth, and encoding—directly impact subsequent transport requirements. For instance, a high-definition security camera will generate significantly more data than a low-resolution sensor, necessitating greater bandwidth for real-time streaming.

- **Compression:** Given the substantial volume of multimedia data, compression is often essential before or during transport. Techniques like H.264/H.265 for video and AAC for audio can significantly reduce data size while maintaining acceptable quality. The choice of compression algorithm affects not only the bandwidth requirements but also the computational load on the devices and the quality of the transmitted content.
- **Storage:** Captured and potentially compressed multimedia data must be stored efficiently and scalably. Storage solutions range from local memory on IoT devices to edge servers and cloud repositories. The choice of storage architecture influences how data is subsequently accessed and transported for processing or streaming.
- **Processing and Analysis:** Multimedia data often requires significant computational resources for analysis to extract meaningful insights. Transporting data to and from processing units, which may reside in the cloud or at the edge (fog computing), is a critical consideration in the design of IoT systems.
- **Interpretation and Assessment:** The results of multimedia analysis need to be transported to user interfaces or decision-making systems. The format and delivery mechanism depend on the specific application requirements and the nature of the insights derived from the data.
- **Security:** Throughout the entire lifecycle, including during transport, security and privacy are paramount concerns, particularly when dealing with sensitive information such as surveillance footage or healthcare data. Secure transport protocols and mechanisms are crucial to protect data integrity and confidentiality.

The Interplay of Transport with MMBD Components

Transport mechanisms do not operate in isolation but are intricately linked with each stage of the MMBD lifecycle. For example, the decision to heavily compress data influences the bandwidth required for transport, while the real-time nature of certain applications imposes stringent latency requirements on the transport protocols employed.

The unstructured and heterogeneous nature of multimedia data adds another layer of complexity to transport solutions. Unlike structured data, multimedia content varies widely in format, size, and characteristics. Transport mechanisms must be adaptable to handle various data formats and capable of managing streams from diverse IoT devices effectively.

Furthermore, metadata plays a crucial role in guiding the processing and transport of multimedia streams. Metadata may include information about the content (e.g., timestamps, location data) and technical specifications (e.g., resolution, frame rate), which can influence transport QoS parameters. For instance, metadata might indicate the priority or real-time sensitivity of a particular data stream, affecting how it is handled during transport.

Integrated Transport Solutions

Effective multimedia transport requires integration with other components of the IoT ecosystem. This integration ensures that transport mechanisms align with the requirements and constraints of the overall system, leading to more efficient and reliable delivery of multimedia content.

For example, a comprehensive solution might incorporate adaptive compression techniques that adjust based on network conditions, prioritized transport for critical data streams, and edge-based processing to reduce the volume of data transmitted to the cloud. By considering the end-to-end flow of multimedia data, such integrated solutions can optimize not only the transport phase but the entire data lifecycle.

In summary, multimedia transport in IoT applications requires a comprehensive understanding of the entire MMBD lifecycle. Transport solutions must be designed and implemented in concert with data acquisition, compression, storage, processing, and security considerations to ensure efficient, reliable, and secure delivery of multimedia information.

Transport Layer Protocols: TCP vs UDP

The choice of transport protocol plays a pivotal role in determining how multimedia data is delivered across networks. Two primary transport layer protocols in the TCP/IP suite are Transmission Control Protocol (TCP) and User Datagram Protocol (UDP). Each has distinct characteristics that make it suitable for different types of multimedia applications in IoT environments.

3.2 TRANSMISSION CONTROL PROTOCOL (TCP)

TCP is a connection-oriented protocol that provides reliable, ordered, and error-checked delivery of data. Its fundamental mechanisms include:

- **Connection Establishment:** Before data transmission begins, TCP establishes a connection between the sender and receiver through a three-way handshake. This process involves the exchange of SYN (synchronize) and ACK (acknowledge) messages to synchronize sequence numbers and establish parameters for the session.
- **Ordered Delivery:** TCP assigns sequence numbers to packets (more precisely, to bytes within the data stream) and ensures they are delivered to the application in the correct order, regardless of the order in which they arrive at the destination.
- **Retransmission:** If a packet is lost or corrupted during transmission, TCP automatically retransmits it. The receiver acknowledges successfully received packets, and the sender maintains a timer for each unacknowledged packet. If an acknowledgment isn't received before the timer expires, the sender assumes the packet was lost and retransmits it.
- **Flow Control:** TCP implements flow control to prevent the sender from overwhelming the receiver with data. The receiver advertises a "window size" indicating how much data it can buffer, and the sender adjusts its transmission rate accordingly.
- **Congestion Control:** To prevent network congestion, TCP employs mechanisms like slow start, congestion avoidance, fast retransmit, and fast recovery. These algorithms dynamically adjust the transmission rate based on network conditions, reducing the rate when congestion is detected and gradually increasing it when the network can handle more traffic.

Advantages and Limitations for Multimedia Transport

While TCP's reliability features are beneficial for ensuring complete and accurate delivery of data, they introduce significant overhead and latency, which can be detrimental to real-time multimedia applications in IoT scenarios. The connection establishment process adds initial delay, and the retransmission of lost packets can cause pauses and disruptions in streaming media.

Moreover, TCP's congestion control mechanisms can reduce the transmission rate during periods of network congestion, potentially leading to buffering or reduced quality in multimedia streams. When an IoT device is streaming video over a congested network, TCP's rate reduction may result in noticeable quality degradation or playback interruptions.

Despite these limitations, TCP is suitable for certain non-real-time multimedia applications where reliability is paramount, and latency is less critical. Examples include downloading multimedia files for offline viewing, buffered video playback, and certain types of data backup or synchronization between IoT devices and cloud storage.

3.3 USER DATAGRAM PROTOCOL (UDP)

In contrast to TCP, UDP is a connectionless protocol that provides a lightweight and faster mechanism for data transmission. Its key characteristics include:

- **No Connection Establishment:** UDP begins data transmission immediately without requiring a handshake, eliminating the initial latency associated with connection establishment.
- **Unordered Delivery:** UDP does not guarantee that packets will arrive in the same order they were sent. Each packet is treated independently, and it's up to the application to handle any necessary reordering.
- **No Retransmission:** UDP does not automatically retransmit lost or corrupted packets. If reliability is required, it must be implemented at the application layer.
- **Minimal Overhead:** UDP has a simpler header and fewer control mechanisms compared to TCP, resulting in lower overhead and reduced processing requirements. This can be especially beneficial for resource-constrained IoT devices.
- **No Congestion Control:** UDP does not implement congestion control mechanisms, allowing applications to maintain their desired transmission rate regardless of network conditions. While this can lead to more consistent multimedia quality, it also risks contributing to network congestion if not managed properly at the application level.

Advantages and Limitations for Multimedia Transport

The reduced latency and overhead of UDP often make it the preferred choice for real-time multimedia applications in IoT environments. For instance, in video surveillance systems or remote monitoring applications, the timely delivery of frames is typically more critical than the guaranteed delivery of every single frame. Minor packet loss might result in occasional visual artifacts but is generally less disruptive than the delays caused by TCP's retransmission mechanisms.

However, UDP's lack of built-in reliability means that applications must implement their own error detection and recovery mechanisms if needed. For example, a smart home security system streaming video over UDP might implement application-level acknowledgments for critical frames or use forward error correction to recover from packet loss without requiring retransmission.

3.4 PROTOCOL SELECTION FOR IOT MULTIMEDIA APPLICATIONS

The choice between TCP and UDP for multimedia transport in IoT applications depends on several factors:

- **Real-time Requirements:** Applications with strict real-time requirements, such as live video monitoring or interactive control systems, generally benefit from UDP's lower latency.
- **Reliability Needs:** Applications where complete and accurate data delivery is critical, such as firmware updates for multimedia-enabled IoT devices, may require TCP's reliability features.
- **Network Conditions:** In highly reliable networks with minimal packet loss, UDP may be sufficient even for applications that require good quality. In contrast, in lossy networks, either TCP or UDP with application-level reliability mechanisms may be necessary.
- **Device Constraints:** Resource-constrained IoT devices may benefit from UDP's lower processing requirements and overhead.

Many modern IoT systems implement hybrid approaches, using UDP for the actual multimedia data transport while employing TCP for control messages and metadata. Additionally, application-layer protocols built on top of UDP can implement selective reliability mechanisms, providing a middle ground between the complete reliability of TCP and the minimal overhead of pure UDP.

Understanding the strengths and limitations of these transport protocols is essential for designing effective multimedia transport solutions in IoT environments. The subsequent chapters will explore how these protocols are utilized within specific streaming technologies and real-time communication frameworks.

3.5 MULTIMEDIA STREAMING TECHNOLOGIES

Multimedia streaming is a technique for delivering audio and video content to users over a network in a continuous flow, without requiring the entire file to be downloaded before playback begins. This capability is particularly crucial for IoT applications that generate large volumes of multimedia data and require real-time monitoring or interaction.

Fundamental Concepts of Streaming

Streaming involves breaking multimedia content into smaller chunks that are transmitted sequentially, allowing the receiver to begin processing and playing the content before all chunks have arrived. This approach offers several advantages over traditional file download methods:

- **Reduced Latency:** Users can begin consuming content almost immediately, rather than waiting for a complete download.
- **Lower Storage Requirements:** The receiver doesn't need to store the entire file, as content can be processed and then discarded as the stream progresses.
- **Adaptability:** Streaming can adapt to changing network conditions by adjusting quality parameters in real-time.
- **Better Resource Utilization:** Network resources are used more efficiently, as only the portions of content that are actually consumed need to be transmitted.

Streaming Models

Several streaming models are commonly employed in IoT multimedia applications:

- **Live Streaming:** Content is captured, encoded, and transmitted in real-time, with minimal delay between capture and playback. This model is common in IoT surveillance systems, traffic monitoring, and live event broadcasting.
- **On-Demand Streaming:** Pre-recorded content is stored and made available for streaming upon request. Examples include archived footage from security cameras or pre-recorded instructional videos from industrial IoT systems.
- **Progressive Download:** A hybrid between download and streaming, where content is downloaded sequentially, and playback can begin once sufficient data has been received. The file continues to download in the background during playback.
- **Adaptive Bitrate Streaming:** Content is encoded at multiple quality levels, and the streaming system dynamically switches between these versions based on network conditions and device capabilities. This approach is particularly valuable in IoT environments with varying connectivity.

Streaming Architectures

The architectural components of a streaming system typically include:

- **Capture Devices:** IoT sensors and devices that generate multimedia content, such as cameras, microphones, and specialized sensors.
- **Encoders:** Software or hardware components that compress raw multimedia data into efficient formats suitable for transmission.
- **Media Servers:** Specialized servers that store multimedia content and manage its delivery to clients. These may include processing capabilities for transcoding or adapting content based on client requirements.
- **Content Delivery Networks (CDNs):** Distributed networks of servers that cache and deliver content from locations closer to end-users, reducing latency and improving scalability.
- **Client Applications:** Software running on end-user devices that receives, decodes, and presents the streamed content. In IoT scenarios, clients might range from dedicated monitoring stations to mobile applications or web interfaces.

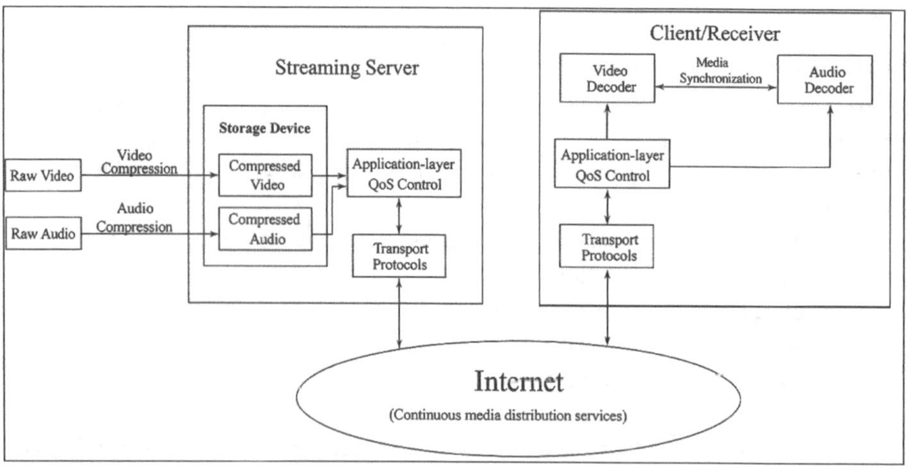

***Figure 3.1:** Multimedia Streaming*

Streaming Technologies in IoT Applications

IoT environments leverage various streaming technologies to meet their specific requirements:

- **Surveillance and Security:** IoT cameras stream live video feeds for monitoring homes, businesses, and public spaces. These systems often employ protocols optimized for security and reliability, with options for encrypted transmission and multi-level access control.
- **Industrial IoT (IIoT):** Video streams from industrial equipment can be used for remote monitoring, predictive maintenance, and quality control. These applications typically require high reliability and may integrate with analytics platforms to detect anomalies or issues in real-time.
- **Healthcare:** Wearable IoT devices capture and stream physiological data, potentially including audio and video for remote consultations or patient monitoring. These streams must be highly secure and reliable, with strict privacy controls.
- **Smart Cities:** IoT sensors deployed across urban environments stream data for traffic management, public safety, and environmental monitoring. These systems often involve multiple coordinated streams that must be synchronized and analyzed collectively.
- **Precision Agriculture:** Drones and ground-based sensors equipped with cameras stream video and images of crops and fields for analysis of plant health, irrigation needs, and other agricultural parameters.

Challenges in IoT Multimedia Streaming

Streaming in IoT environments presents several unique challenges:

- **Heterogeneity:** IoT ecosystems involve diverse devices with varying capabilities for multimedia capture, encoding, and transmission. Streaming solutions must accommodate this heterogeneity while maintaining interoperability.
- **Resource Constraints:** Many IoT devices operate with limited processing power, memory, and energy. Streaming implementations must be optimized to function within these constraints while delivering acceptable quality.
- **Dynamic Network Conditions:** IoT devices often connect through wireless networks with fluctuating bandwidth, latency, and reliability. Streaming technologies must adapt to these changing conditions to maintain continuous service.
- **Scale:** IoT deployments can involve hundreds or thousands of streaming devices, placing significant demands on network infrastructure and management systems.

As IoT applications continue to expand, streaming technologies will play an increasingly critical role in enabling real-time monitoring, analysis, and interaction with the physical world. The following chapters will explore how these streaming capabilities are enhanced through quality of experience considerations, network optimization techniques, and specialized protocols for real-time communication.

3.6 ACCESSING AUDIO AND VIDEO FROM WEB SERVER AND MEDIA SERVER

Audio and video streaming play a vital role in modern web applications, entertainment, and multimedia services. Understanding how media is accessed and delivered from both web and media servers is crucial for ensuring efficient playback and streaming. A **web server**, such as Apache or Nginx, serves static media files via HTTP or HTTPS. These files can either be downloaded or streamed directly. Users can access media through direct URLs, such as https://example.com/media/video.mp4, which can be embedded in HTML using <audio> or <video> tags. Media delivery from web servers can occur through **progressive download**, where the file is downloaded in chunks as it plays, allowing users to seek within already downloaded parts. However, **streaming** offers real-time playback without requiring users to download the entire file, using specialized protocols like HLS, DASH, or RTMP.

A **media server**, in contrast, is designed for optimized media streaming and supports multiple simultaneous users. It utilizes various streaming protocols, including **HLS (HTTP Live Streaming)** for Apple devices, **MPEG-DASH** for adaptive bitrate streaming, **RTMP (Real-Time Messaging Protocol)** for low-latency live streaming, and **WebRTC** for real-time communication. Media server software such as **Wowza Streaming Engine**, **Red5**, **NGINX with the RTMP module**, and **FFmpeg** provide robust solutions for streaming and transcoding. Compared to web servers, media servers enable smoother playback, adaptive bitrate streaming, and lower latency, making them ideal for large-scale live and on-demand streaming services.

While web servers are suitable for hosting static media files and progressive downloads, media servers are optimized for real-time streaming, making them more efficient for delivering high-quality video content. A key difference lies in the supported protocols and performance—web servers use HTTP/HTTPS, whereas media servers support advanced streaming protocols like HLS and RTMP, ensuring a better user experience. Security measures such as **Digital Rights Management (DRM)**, **token authentication**, and **encryption (AES-128, Widevine, FairPlay)** help protect media content from unauthorized access and piracy.

3.7 REMOVING JITTER AT THE RECEIVER

Jitter, or variations in packet arrival time, can disrupt the smooth playback of multimedia streams. To counteract jitter effects, buffering techniques are commonly employed at the receiver.

A jitter buffer temporarily stores incoming packets before playback, allowing the system to compensate for irregular arrival patterns. By introducing a controlled delay, the buffer can smooth out timing variations and present a consistent stream to the decoder. The design of effective jitter buffers involves several considerations:

- **Buffer Size:** A larger buffer can absorb greater amounts of jitter but introduces higher latency. A smaller buffer reduces latency but may be less effective at handling significant jitter. The optimal size depends on the application requirements and network characteristics.
- **Adaptive Buffering:** Rather than using a fixed buffer size, adaptive algorithms dynamically adjust the buffer based on observed network conditions. These algorithms monitor jitter patterns and adjust the buffer size to maintain an optimal balance between smoothness and latency.
- **Playout Delay Adjustment:** Some systems dynamically adjust the playout delay during natural pauses in content (e.g., silence periods in audio) to minimize the perceived impact of buffering.

- **Priority-Based Buffering:** Not all multimedia packets are equally important. Buffering strategies can prioritize key frames or critical audio segments to ensure they are available for playback even under challenging network conditions.

In IoT applications, effective jitter buffering must often be implemented with consideration for device constraints, especially limited memory and processing capabilities in edge devices.

Packet Loss Recovery Mechanisms

Packet loss is an inevitable phenomenon in network communications that can significantly impact multimedia quality. Several strategies can be employed to recover from packet loss or mitigate its effects:

Forward Error Correction (FEC)

FEC techniques add redundant data to the original stream, allowing the receiver to reconstruct lost packets without requiring retransmission. Common approaches include:

- **Parity-based FEC:** Simple schemes where parity bits are added to detect and potentially correct errors
- **Reed-Solomon Codes:** More powerful error correction codes that can recover from multiple packet losses
- **Fountain Codes:** Rateless erasure codes that generate an unlimited number of encoding symbols, requiring only a minimum number to be received for successful decoding

Retransmission Schemes

While traditional Automatic Repeat reQuest (ARQ) mechanisms may be too slow for real-time streaming, modified approaches can be effective:

- **Selective Retransmission:** Only requesting retransmission of the most critical lost packets
- **Time-Constrained Retransmission:** Setting deadlines beyond which retransmitted packets are no longer useful
- **Hybrid ARQ:** Combining FEC with retransmission to optimize recovery efficiency

Error Concealment

When packet recovery is not possible, error concealment techniques at the decoder attempt to minimize the perceptual impact of lost data:

- **Audio Concealment:** Methods include packet repetition, interpolation between adjacent packets, or model-based synthesis
- **Video Concealment:** Techniques such as frame copying, motion-compensated interpolation, or spatial interpolation within a frame

Interleaving

This technique rearranges data before transmission so that related content is spread across multiple packets. When a burst loss occurs, the damage is distributed across the content rather than concentrated in one area, making concealment more effective.

Adapting to Bandwidth Constraints

Limited or fluctuating bandwidth is a common challenge in IoT environments. Several approaches can help multimedia applications adapt to these constraints:

- **Scalable Coding:** Multimedia content is encoded in layers, with a base layer providing minimum quality and enhancement layers improving quality when bandwidth permits. Receivers can decode whatever layers they receive, ensuring some level of service even under severe bandwidth limitations.
- **Multiple Description Coding:** Content is encoded into multiple complementary descriptions, each providing an acceptable quality level if received alone. Quality improves as more descriptions are received, providing graceful degradation under packet loss or bandwidth constraints.
- **Bitrate Adaptation:** Streaming systems dynamically adjust the bitrate based on observed bandwidth. This can involve switching between pre-encoded versions (as in adaptive bitrate streaming) or dynamic encoding parameter adjustments.
- **Content-Aware Compression:** Adapt compression based on content characteristics and importance. For example, regions of interest in surveillance video might be encoded at higher quality than background areas.
- **Transcoding at Network Edges:** Deploy transcoding capabilities at edge nodes to adapt high-quality streams to the bandwidth constraints of specific network segments or devices.

Cross-Layer Approaches to Network Impairment Handling

While traditional networking follows a strict layered approach, cross-layer design—where information is shared between protocol layers—can be particularly effective for multimedia transport in challenging IoT environments:

- **Application-Aware Networking:** Lower layers (transport, network) use information about application requirements to optimize their behavior. For example, knowing which packets contain critical frames can influence scheduling and routing decisions.
- **Network-Aware Applications:** Applications adapt their behavior based on information about network conditions. For example, an IoT camera might adjust its capture parameters based on available bandwidth.
- **Joint Optimization:** Simultaneous adaptation across multiple layers to optimize overall performance. For example, coordinating application-level encoding parameters, transport protocol behavior, and link-layer error control.
- **Middleware Approaches:** Intermediate software layers that facilitate information sharing between traditional protocol layers while maintaining modularity and compatibility with existing systems.

By implementing these techniques for handling network impairments, IoT multimedia applications can maintain acceptable quality even under challenging network conditions. The specific combination of approaches depends on the application requirements, device capabilities, and network characteristics of the particular IoT deployment.

3.8 INTERACTIVE VS NON-INTERACTIVE MULTIMEDIA TRANSPORT

Multimedia applications in IoT environments can be broadly classified into interactive and non-interactive categories, each imposing different demands on the underlying transport mechanisms. Understanding these distinctions is crucial for designing effective transport solutions that meet application-specific requirements.

Characteristics of Non-Interactive Multimedia

Non-interactive multimedia applications involve one-way communication where users passively consume content without directly controlling its flow in real-time. Examples include:

- **Video Surveillance:** Security cameras streaming footage to monitoring stations or storage servers
- **Environmental Monitoring:** Sensors capturing and transmitting periodic multimedia samples of natural phenomena
- **Digital Signage:** IoT displays receiving and showing content from central management systems
- **Background Audio:** Ambient sound or music delivery systems

Key characteristics of non-interactive multimedia transport include:

- **Latency Tolerance:** While excessive delays are undesirable, non-interactive applications can typically tolerate higher latency than interactive ones. A delay of several seconds may be acceptable for surveillance video that is being recorded rather than actively monitored.
- **Buffering Capability:** Receivers can implement substantial buffering to smooth out network variations without significantly impacting the user experience. This allows for more stable playback under varying network conditions.
- **Quality Prioritization:** In bandwidth-constrained scenarios, non-interactive applications often prioritize quality over timeliness. For example, a higher resolution with occasional pauses might be preferable to continuous but heavily degraded video.
- **Asymmetric Communication:** The data flow is predominantly in one direction, from the source to the consumer, with minimal return traffic for control messages.

Characteristics of Interactive Multimedia

Interactive multimedia applications involve bidirectional communication with real-time interaction between participants or between users and systems. Examples include:

- **Video Conferencing:** Real-time audio and video communication between multiple participants
- Remote Control Systems

Transcoding: Handling Heterogeneous Multimedia Data

The IoT landscape features a diverse array of devices producing multimedia data in various formats, resolutions, frame rates, and encoding schemes. Transcoding plays a crucial role in ensuring interoperability and efficient data transport across this heterogeneous environment.

Purpose and Applications of Transcoding

Transcoding is the process of converting multimedia content from one format or encoding to another, serving several critical purposes in IoT multimedia transport:

- **Device Compatibility:** Target devices (e.g., smartphones, smart TVs, web browsers) typically support only a limited set of multimedia codecs and formats. Transcoding ensures that streamed content can be properly rendered on receiving devices with different capabilities.
- **Network Adaptation:** When network bandwidth is limited or variable, transcoding allows content to be converted to a lower bitrate or resolution, ensuring smooth delivery despite constrained resources. This capability forms the foundation of adaptive bitrate streaming (ABR) techniques widely used in modern multimedia delivery systems.
- **Processing Standardization:** For analytical tasks, having all multimedia data in a consistent format simplifies processing pipelines. Transcoding can normalize heterogeneous inputs into a standardized format suitable for algorithmic analysis.

3.9 TRANSCODING CONSIDERATIONS IN IOT

Resource Requirements: Transcoding is computationally intensive, requiring significant processing power and energy. In IoT environments with resource-constrained devices, careful consideration must be given to where transcoding occurs within the network topology.

- **Transcoding Locations:** Source Transcoding: Performed at the origin before streaming, typically on servers with sufficient computational resources - Network Transcoding: Executed by intermediate nodes (e.g., edge servers) to adapt content based on network conditions - Destination Transcoding: Carried out by the receiving device, though less common for real-time applications due to resource limitations
- **Challenges:** The increasing diversity of multimedia data sources in IoT environments underscores the need for efficient and scalable transcoding solutions that can operate within the constraints of IoT infrastructures.

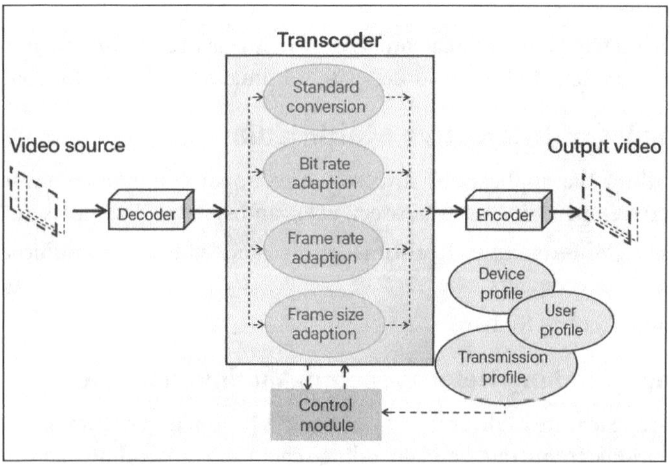

Figure 3.2: *Architecture of video transcoding*

Real-Time Streaming Protocols for IoT

Real-time multimedia streaming in IoT environments requires specialized protocols designed to address the unique requirements of low latency, synchronization, and control. Several protocols have emerged to fulfill these needs.

Real-time Transport Protocol (RTP)

RTP is a transport protocol providing end-to-end delivery services for real-time data, such as audio and video, over IP networks. It typically operates over UDP to minimize latency and offers several essential features:

Key Features:

- Payload Type Identification: Indicates the format of the multimedia data being transported
- Sequence Numbering: Enables receivers to detect packet loss and reorder packets when necessary
- Timestamping: Provides timing information for synchronizing audio and video streams and calculating jitter

Limitations: RTP itself does not guarantee Quality of Service (QoS); it relies on lower-layer protocols for packet delivery and associated control protocols for session management and QoS feedback.

Real-Time Streaming Protocol (RTSP)

RTSP is an application-layer control protocol designed for establishing and controlling media sessions between endpoints. It functions as a "network remote control" for multimedia servers, allowing clients to initiate and direct streaming media delivery.

Key Features:

- Employs a client-server model with HTTP-like messaging
- Supports commands such as SETUP, PLAY, PAUSE, and TEARDOWN
- Can utilize either TCP or UDP as its underlying transport protocol

Protocol Integration: RTSP typically works in conjunction with RTP, where RTSP manages the streaming session while RTP transports the actual multimedia data. For example, a client might use RTSP to request a specific video stream from a media server, specify transport parameters (e.g., RTP over UDP), and then receive the video packets via RTP.

Practical Applications

These protocols find widespread use in IoT applications requiring real-time multimedia transport, such as: Voice over IP (VoIP) services - Security camera feeds - Telemedicine systems - Industrial monitoring and control systems

Energy Considerations in Multimedia Transport

Energy efficiency represents a critical concern in IoT environments, particularly for battery-powered devices that generate and transmit multimedia data. The energy-intensive nature of multimedia transport necessitates careful consideration of power consumption at all stages of the data lifecycle.

SUMMARY

The transmission of data is of utmost importance in multimedia networking and can be done through end-to-end solutions ensuring a balance between quality and efficiency. The protocols' robustness like TCP and UDP rely on minimal intervention which is a hallmark of the laissez-faire approach. UDP is preferred during multimedia streaming because it has low latency and overhead, while TCP guarantees dependable delivery. Streaming multimedia involves retrieving audio and video content from web servers and dedicated media servers. The FEC techniques, in combination with interleaving, improve data integrity, while jitter removal and packet loss reconstruction enhance the playback performance. Interactive real-time communication and on-demand content require adaptive handling due to their non-interactivity. Network and device dependant content adaptation is done through transcoding. For optimal performance, RTSP and RTP/RTCP protocols ensure effective synchronization, control, and feedback mechanisms aiding in effective multimedia communication. The integration of these technologies improve the experience and delivery of multimedia applications over networks.

4

UNIT

Evolution Embedded Internet

4.1 INTRODUCTION TO THE EMBEDDED INTERNET AND ITS TRANSFORMATION

The internet has evolved dramatically since its inception, transitioning from a network primarily connecting desktop computers to one that now encompasses billions of embedded devices. This evolution represents a fundamental shift in how we conceptualize connectivity and computing power within our physical environment.

The Foundational Concepts of the Embedded Internet

The embedded internet refers to the integration of internet connectivity into everyday objects and devices that traditionally functioned without such connectivity. Unlike traditional computing devices, embedded internet devices are typically designed for specific functions, operate with limited resources, and often need to function autonomously for extended periods. The evolution of microprocessors, wireless communication technologies, and energy-efficient design has enabled this transformation, allowing computing power to be embedded into an increasingly diverse range of objects.

The Rise of the Internet of Things (IoT) as a Catalyst for Evolution

The Internet of Things (IoT) represents the most significant manifestation of the embedded internet concept. IoT can be defined as a network of physical objects embedded with sensors, software, and connectivity that enables these objects to connect and exchange data. The key characteristics of IoT include:

- **Unique identifiers (UIDs)**: Each device possesses a unique identifier that distinguishes it within the network.
- **Connectivity**: Devices can connect to the internet or to other devices, forming networks of varying complexity.
- **Physical objects with digital presence**: Everyday objects become "smart" through embedded technology.
- **Data exchange without human intervention**: Devices communicate autonomously, often making decisions based on predefined parameters or machine learning algorithms.

The proliferation of IoT devices has been remarkable, with estimates suggesting tens of billions of connected devices worldwide. This expansion has fundamentally changed how we interact with technology, moving from deliberate human-computer interactions to ambient computing environments where processing happens continuously and often invisibly.

The Emergence of Multimedia Big Data (MMBD) in the IoT Era

A critical consequence of the IoT revolution has been the unprecedented generation of data, particularly multimedia data. Multimedia Big Data (MMBD) refers to the vast amounts of unstructured data in various formats (images, audio, video, text) generated by globally distributed devices.

The characteristics of MMBD include:

- **Volume**: The sheer quantity of data generated exceeds traditional processing capabilities.
- **Variety**: Data comes in multiple formats and structures, complicating unified analysis.
- **Unstructured nature**: Unlike traditional database entries, multimedia data lacks predetermined organization.
- **Real-time processing requirements**: Many applications require immediate analysis and response.

The combination of IoT and MMBD has created unique computing challenges. Traditional data processing approaches are often inadequate for handling the scale and complexity of data generated by IoT devices. This has necessitated innovations in data compression, transmission, storage, and analysis techniques.

The "Network of Networks" Paradigm

The embedded internet can be conceptualized as a "network of networks," where various specialized networks (home automation, industrial control systems, vehicle networks, etc.) interconnect and share data. This hierarchical and heterogeneous structure adds complexity to the management and optimization of the overall system.

The Scarcity of Resources in the MMBD Context

Despite advances in computing power and storage, the explosion of multimedia data has created persistent resource scarcity issues:

- **Storage limitations**: The volume of generated data often exceeds available storage capacity.
- **Bandwidth constraints**: Transmitting multimedia data requires significant bandwidth, creating bottlenecks in many applications.
- **Energy constraints**: Many IoT devices operate on limited power sources, making energy efficiency crucial.

These constraints have driven the development of efficient compression techniques and intelligent data management strategies that balance information preservation with resource utilization.

4.2 MOBILE CROWD SENSING

As the embedded internet continues to evolve, Mobile Crowd Sensing (MCS) has emerged as a powerful paradigm that leverages the sensing capabilities of mobile devices to collect and analyze data about people and their environments. This approach is particularly relevant in the IoT context, where the ubiquity of sensor-equipped devices creates unprecedented opportunities for distributed data collection.

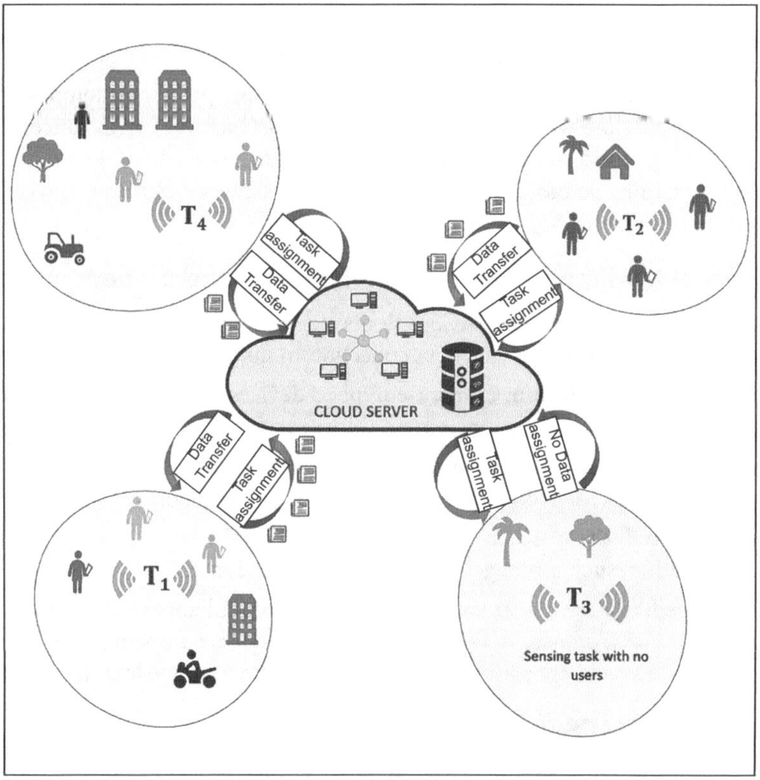

Figure 4.1: *Mobile Crowd Sensing*

Understanding Mobile Crowd Sensing Principles

Mobile Crowd Sensing involves the collection of data from a distributed network of sensing devices, typically carried or operated by humans. Key principles of MCS include:

- **Participatory sensing**: Users actively engage in the data collection process by deliberately contributing sensor data.
- **Opportunistic sensing**: Data is collected automatically without user intervention as devices move through different environments.
- **Human-as-a-sensor**: People themselves act as sensors, providing observations and subjective assessments that complement machine-generated data.
- **Incentivization mechanisms**: Various approaches to motivate participation, from gamification to monetary rewards.

The integration of MCS with IoT creates a powerful synergy, combining the mobility and human context of crowd sensing with the pervasiveness and autonomy of IoT systems.

IoT Devices and Sensors as Distributed Data Sources

Within the MCS paradigm, IoT devices serve as distributed data sources that can capture a wide range of phenomena:

- **Environmental parameters**: Temperature, humidity, air quality, noise levels, etc.
- **Location and movement data**: GPS coordinates, acceleration, orientation.

- **Biometric information**: Heart rate, steps, sleep patterns.
- **Media content**: Images, videos, audio recordings.

The distributed nature of these data sources allows for spatial and temporal coverage that would be impossible with traditional sensing infrastructure. For instance, air quality monitoring through fixed stations provides detailed data at specific points but misses the fine-grained variations across urban environments that can be captured through mobile sensors carried by citizens.

Generation of Multimedia Data Through Mobile and Embedded Devices

A distinguishing feature of modern MCS systems is their ability to generate rich multimedia data. This capability has transformed data collection in numerous ways:

- **Visual documentation**: Camera-equipped devices can capture images and videos of environmental conditions, urban infrastructure, or events of interest.
- **Audio sampling**: Microphones can record ambient noise levels, specific sounds (e.g., bird calls for ecological monitoring), or verbal reports.
- **Augmented data**: Basic sensor readings can be enriched with contextual information, such as images annotated with location and time stamps.

This multimedia data provides contextual richness that enhances the value of numerical sensor readings. For instance, a report of road damage accompanied by a geotagged photograph provides far more actionable information than a simple location marker.

Applications of MCS in IoT Scenarios

The combination of MCS and IoT has enabled innovative applications across various domains:

- **Environmental monitoring**: Tracking pollution levels, noise pollution, or water quality through distributed sensing.
- **Smart cities**: Monitoring traffic conditions, identifying infrastructure issues, or assessing the utilization of public spaces.
- **Public health surveillance**: Tracking the spread of diseases, monitoring allergen levels, or assessing the impact of environmental factors on health.
- **Emergency response**: Gathering real-time information during disasters or critical events to support decision-making.

These applications leverage the ubiquity of IoT devices and the mobility of humans to collect data that would be impractical to gather through traditional means.

Challenges in Data Reliability and Efficient Scalability

Despite its potential, MCS in IoT contexts faces significant challenges:

- **Data quality and reliability**: Ensuring the accuracy of data collected by diverse devices with varying capabilities and calibration.
- **Privacy concerns**: Protecting sensitive information while enabling useful data collection.
- **Efficient data transmission**: Minimizing bandwidth usage when transmitting multimedia data from resource-constrained devices.

- **Scalability**: Managing and processing the vast amounts of data generated by distributed sensing devices.
- **Heterogeneity**: Handling data from devices with different specifications, capabilities, and formats.

Addressing these challenges requires innovations in data validation techniques, privacy-preserving data collection methods, and efficient data aggregation and transmission protocols tailored to the characteristics of MCS in IoT environments.

4.3 PERSPECTIVE PROTOCOL STACK FOR WIRELESS IoT NETWORKS

The unique characteristics and constraints of IoT devices necessitate specialized networking approaches that differ significantly from those used in traditional internet communication. This chapter explores the protocol stack considerations for wireless IoT networks, with a particular focus on energy efficiency and resource optimization.

Traditional Protocol Stacks and Their Limitations

Traditional internet protocol stacks, such as the TCP/IP model, were designed for devices with reliable power sources, substantial computing capabilities, and relatively stable connections. However, these protocol stacks present several limitations when applied to IoT contexts:

- **Overhead**: Protocols like TCP include substantial header information and handshaking procedures that consume precious bandwidth.
- **Energy consumption**: Continuous connection maintenance and acknowledgment mechanisms drain battery life.
- **Memory requirements**: Full implementation of standard protocols requires significant memory resources.
- **Processing demands**: Complex protocol processing taxes limited CPU capabilities.

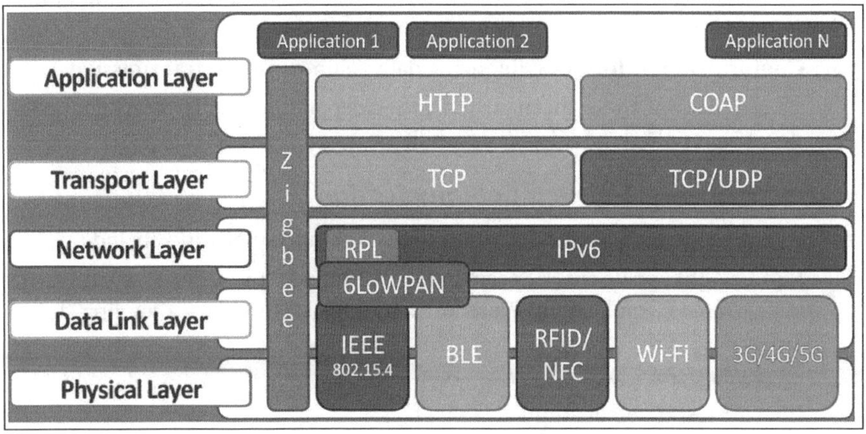

Figure 4.2: Wireless Protocol for Iot

These limitations have driven the development of specialized protocol stacks that are optimized for the constrained resources of IoT devices while maintaining essential functionality.

Energy-Efficient Communication Protocols for IoT

Energy efficiency has emerged as a primary design consideration for IoT communication protocols, given that many devices operate on batteries or harvested energy. Research in this area has focused on several key approaches:

Designing Energy-Efficient Protocols

Energy-efficient protocol design incorporates techniques such as:

- **Reduced header sizes**: Minimizing packet overhead to decrease transmission energy.
- **Simplified handshaking**: Streamlining connection establishment and maintenance.
- **Adaptive duty cycling**: Allowing devices to sleep during periods of inactivity.
- **Cross-layer optimization**: Coordinating decisions across protocol layers to minimize overall energy usage.

These design principles have influenced the development of specialized IoT protocols at various layers of the network stack.

Survey of Proposed Mechanisms for Energy Conservation

Research literature has proposed numerous mechanisms for conserving energy in wireless IoT networks:

- **Low-power listening**: Devices periodically sample the channel for activity rather than continuously listening.
- **Contention-based MAC protocols**: Reducing energy spent on channel access through efficient medium sharing.
- **Cluster-based routing**: Organizing devices into clusters to minimize transmission distances and aggregate data.
- **Data aggregation and fusion**: Combining related data to reduce the number of transmissions.
- **Compression techniques**: Reducing data volume prior to transmission.

The effectiveness of these mechanisms varies depending on the specific application scenario, network topology, and device capabilities.

Solutions for Energy-Efficient Communication

Practical solutions for energy-efficient communication in IoT networks include:

- **Lightweight protocols**: Specialized alternatives to TCP/IP such as CoAP (Constrained Application Protocol) and MQTT (Message Queuing Telemetry Transport).
- **6LoWPAN**: IPv6 over Low-Power Wireless Personal Area Networks, which adapts IPv6 for resource-constrained devices.
- **RPL**: Routing Protocol for Low-Power and Lossy Networks, designed specifically for IoT contexts.
- **Bluetooth Low Energy (BLE)**: A power-efficient version of Bluetooth designed for IoT applications.

These solutions balance functionality with energy efficiency, enabling practical deployment of IoT systems with reasonable battery life.

Wireless Networking Aspects of IoT Energy Conservation

Different wireless networking technologies offer varying trade-offs in terms of range, bandwidth, and energy consumption:

- **Wireless Wide Area Networks (WWAN)**: Technologies like NB-IoT and LTE-M provide long-range connectivity but typically consume more power.
- **Wireless Local Area Networks (WLAN)**: Wi-Fi offers high bandwidth but has relatively high-power requirements, though low-power variants are emerging.
- **Wireless Personal Area Networks (WPAN)**: Technologies like ZigBee and Thread provide energy-efficient communication over shorter distances.

The selection of appropriate wireless technology depends on the specific requirements of the IoT application, including coverage area, data rate, and energy constraints.

Converged Fiber-Wireless (Fi-Wi) Access Networks

For large-scale IoT deployments, converged Fiber-Wireless (Fi-Wi) access networks present an attractive solution:

- **Fiber backbone**: Provides high capacity for backhaul traffic.
- **Wireless last-mile**: Enables flexible connection of distributed IoT devices.
- **Hierarchical architecture**: Supports efficient data aggregation and processing.

This hybrid approach combines the high capacity of fiber optic networks with the flexibility and deployment ease of wireless technologies, creating an infrastructure well-suited to the demands of IoT applications.

Network Resources and Multimedia Traffic

Processing multimedia traffic in IoT networks requires careful consideration of network resources:

- **Bandwidth allocation**: Prioritizing critical data streams while managing less time-sensitive traffic.
- **Quality of Service (QoS)**: Ensuring appropriate service levels for different types of multimedia content.
- **Edge processing**: Reducing network load by processing data closer to its source.
- **Adaptive compression**: Adjusting compression levels based on available network resources.

These strategies help balance the competing demands of multimedia traffic quality and resource conservation in IoT networks.

4.4 WIRELESS SENSOR NETWORKS (WSNS) AND THEIR INTEGRATION WITH THE INTERNET OF THINGS

Wireless Sensor Networks (WSNs) represent one of the fundamental building blocks of the Internet of Things ecosystem. These specialized networks of distributed sensors have evolved from isolated systems to integral components of the broader IoT infrastructure, enabling comprehensive environmental monitoring and data collection.

Fundamental Concepts of Wireless Sensor Networks

A Wireless Sensor Network consists of spatially distributed autonomous devices (sensor nodes) that cooperatively monitor physical or environmental conditions. The core characteristics of WSNs include:

- **Sensor nodes**: Small, typically low-cost devices equipped with sensing capabilities, limited processing power, wireless communication, and power sources.
- **Self-organization**: Nodes automatically establish and maintain network connectivity.
- **Multi-hop communication**: Data is relayed through intermediate nodes to reach a central collection point or gateway.
- **Resource constraints**: Limited energy, processing capability, memory, and communication bandwidth.

WSNs are designed to gather data about their surroundings and transmit this information to central processing systems where it can be analyzed and acted upon. The architecture typically includes:

- **Sensor nodes**: Responsible for data acquisition and initial processing.
- **Sink nodes/gateways**: Collect data from multiple sensor nodes and facilitate communication with external networks.
- **Management systems**: Process, store, and analyze the collected data.

WSNs as a Key Component of the IoT Infrastructure

The integration of WSNs into the IoT ecosystem transforms isolated sensing systems into components of a comprehensive, internet-connected infrastructure. This integration occurs in several ways:

- **IP-enabled sensors**: Equipping sensor nodes with IP networking capabilities to enable direct internet connectivity.
- **Gateway-mediated connectivity**: Using gateway devices to bridge between WSN protocols and internet protocols.
- **Cloud integration**: Connecting WSNs to cloud platforms for data storage, processing, and visualization.
- **Standardized interfaces**: Developing common APIs and data formats to facilitate interoperability.

This integration enables sensor data to flow seamlessly into broader IoT applications, combining with other data sources to create comprehensive views of physical environments and processes.

Application Areas of WSNs in IoT

The combination of WSNs and IoT has enabled transformative applications across numerous domains:

- **Environmental monitoring**: Tracking parameters like temperature, humidity, air quality, or water conditions across wide areas.
- **Precision agriculture**: Monitoring soil moisture, nutrient levels, and crop health to optimize irrigation and fertilization.

- **Industrial monitoring**: Supervising equipment operation, detecting anomalies, and predicting maintenance needs.
- **Smart buildings**: Optimizing energy usage, ensuring comfort, and enhancing security through distributed sensing.
- **Healthcare**: Remote patient monitoring, activity tracking, and ambient assisted living for elderly or vulnerable individuals.
- **Urban infrastructure**: Monitoring structural health of bridges, buildings, and other critical infrastructure.

These applications leverage the distributed nature of WSNs to collect fine-grained data across space and time, providing insights that would be impossible with isolated sensors or periodic manual measurements.

Research Challenges in WSNs for IoT

Despite significant advances, several challenges remain in the effective integration of WSNs into IoT systems:

Routing Issues

Efficient routing of data through WSNs remains challenging due to:

- **Dynamic topologies**: Nodes may join, leave, or move, requiring adaptive routing strategies.
- **Energy constraints**: Routing protocols must balance data delivery reliability with energy conservation.
- **Heterogeneous capabilities**: Networks often include nodes with varying transmission ranges, processing power, and energy reserves.
- **Scalability concerns**: Routing approaches must function effectively as networks grow in size.

Research continues to explore hierarchical, geographic, and content-centric routing approaches that address these challenges.

Network Security

Security is particularly critical for WSNs integrated into IoT systems:

- **Resource-constrained security**: Implementing cryptographic protections on limited hardware.
- **Physical vulnerability**: Nodes are often deployed in accessible locations where they may be tampered with.
- **Attack surfaces**: Distributed nature creates multiple potential entry points for attackers.
- **Data integrity**: Ensuring measurements haven't been falsified or corrupted.

Addressing these security challenges requires lightweight cryptographic protocols, intrusion detection systems, and secure key management approaches tailored to the constraints of WSN environments.

Energy Conservation

Energy remains the most critical constraint for most WSN deployments:

- **Battery limitations**: Many deployments rely on batteries with finite capacity.
- **Replacement difficulties**: Sensors may be deployed in remote or inaccessible locations.
- **Operational longevity**: Applications often require years of unattended operation.

Research in this area focuses on energy-efficient communication protocols, duty cycling approaches, and algorithmic optimizations to extend node lifetime.

Energy Harvesting Methods in Large-Scale IoT Systems with WSNs

To address energy constraints, energy harvesting techniques have gained prominence in WSN research:

- **Solar energy**: Photovoltaic cells convert light into electrical energy.
- **Thermal energy**: Thermoelectric generators exploit temperature differentials.
- **Vibrational energy**: Piezoelectric materials convert mechanical vibrations into electricity.
- **RF energy harvesting**: Capturing energy from ambient radio frequency signals.
- **Wind energy**: Micro-turbines generate power from air movement.

These approaches aim to make sensor nodes energetically self-sufficient, enabling truly maintenance-free deployments over extended periods. Energy harvesting techniques are especially valuable for remote deployments where battery replacement is impractical.

Examples of WSN-Based Applications for Data Collection

Several successful deployments illustrate the potential of WSNs in IoT contexts:

- **Agricultural monitoring systems**: Networks of soil moisture sensors, weather stations, and crop health monitors providing data for precision farming.
- **Urban environmental monitoring**: Distributed air quality and noise pollution sensors throughout cities providing real-time pollution maps.
- **Wildlife tracking networks**: Sensors deployed in natural habitats to monitor animal movements and environmental conditions.
- **Industrial condition monitoring**: Vibration, temperature, and acoustic sensors monitoring equipment health in factories and plants.
- **Building management systems**: Occupancy, temperature, and air quality sensors optimizing comfort and energy usage in commercial buildings.

These examples demonstrate how WSNs serve as the sensory foundation of IoT systems, providing the real-world data that drives intelligent decision-making and automation.

4.5 MACHINE-TO-MACHINE (M2M) COMMUNICATIONS AND THE EMBEDDED INTERNET

Machine-to-Machine (M2M) communication represents a fundamental paradigm shift in how devices interact, moving from human-mediated exchanges to autonomous device interactions. This shift is central to the evolution of the embedded internet and the Internet of Things, enabling scalable, efficient, and automated systems.

Defining Machine-to-Machine Communication in the Context of the Embedded Internet

M2M communication refers to direct communication between devices without human intervention. In the context of the embedded internet, M2M communication involves:

- **Autonomous interactions**: Devices communicate and make decisions without requiring human oversight or intervention.
- **Standardized protocols**: Common communication frameworks enable interoperability across different devices and manufacturers.
- **Structured data exchange**: Information is formatted in ways that machines can readily process and respond to.
- **Event-driven communication**: Devices initiate communication based on predefined triggers or conditions.

Unlike traditional human-oriented communication systems, M2M communications are optimized for efficiency, reliability, and automation rather than user experience or interface design.

The Inherent Nature of M2M Communication Within IoT

M2M communication is intrinsic to the IoT concept, as it enables the autonomous interaction that defines truly "smart" environments:

- **Seamless integration**: Devices from different domains can communicate and coordinate their actions.
- **Scalability**: Systems can grow to include thousands or millions of devices while maintaining functionality.
- **Reduced latency**: Direct device-to-device communication eliminates human processing delays.
- **Continuous operation**: Systems can function 24/7 without human scheduling or intervention.

This autonomous communication capability transforms collections of connected devices into cohesive systems that can respond to changing conditions, optimize resource usage, and deliver services with minimal human oversight.

M2M Communications as a Driver for Big Data Generation

The proliferation of M2M communications has accelerated the generation of data, contributing significantly to the big data phenomenon:

- **Continuous monitoring**: Devices constantly measure and report on their environment or status.
- **High frequency sampling**: Many applications require frequent or real-time data collection.
- **Distributed sources**: Data is generated from geographically dispersed devices.
- **Diverse data types**: M2M systems generate structured, semi-structured, and unstructured data.

The volume and velocity of data generated by M2M communications create both opportunities and challenges. On one hand, this data enables unprecedented insights and automation capabilities. On the other hand, it necessitates advanced data management and analysis approaches to extract value from the massive data streams.

The Role of Sensor Devices in Generating Data for Big Data Applications

Sensor devices serve as the primary data sources in M2M systems, converting physical phenomena into digital information:

- **Environmental sensors**: Measure parameters like temperature, humidity, light levels, or air quality.
- **Motion and position sensors**: Detect movement, orientation, or location.
- **Biometric sensors**: Monitor physiological parameters such as heart rate or blood pressure.
- **Industrial sensors**: Track equipment performance, vibration, or operational parameters.
- **Image and audio sensors**: Capture visual and acoustic information about the environment.

These sensors generate diverse data streams that, when aggregated and analyzed, can reveal patterns and insights that drive decision-making in IoT applications. The data generated by these sensors is often multimedia in nature, combining numerical readings with contextual information such as images, audio, or location data.

Scalable M2M Routing Protocols for Energy-Efficient IoT Wireless Applications

As M2M networks grow in scale, efficient routing becomes critical for maintaining performance while conserving energy:

- **Hierarchical protocols**: Organize devices into clusters to reduce routing complexity and transmission distances.
- **Location-aware routing**: Leverage geographic information to optimize path selection.
- **Content-centric approaches**: Route based on the type of information rather than specific device addresses.
- **Context-adaptive protocols**: Adjust routing strategies based on network conditions and application requirements.

These protocols aim to balance several competing objectives:

- **Minimizing energy consumption**: Extending the operational life of battery-powered devices.
- **Ensuring reliability**: Maintaining consistent data delivery despite device failures or communication interference.
- **Supporting scalability**: Functioning effectively as the network grows to include more devices.
- **Adapting to dynamics**: Handling changes in network topology as devices join, leave, or move.

The development of efficient M2M routing protocols remains an active area of research, with particular focus on approaches that can support the massive scale and heterogeneity of IoT deployments while respecting the energy constraints of embedded devices.

4.6 NANO NETWORKS AND THEIR POTENTIAL ROLE IN THE IoT EVOLUTION

While the provided sources do not explicitly detail nano networks, this concept represents an emerging frontier in the evolution of embedded internet technologies. Nano networks—communication networks composed of nano-scale devices—could potentially extend the reach of IoT into previously inaccessible domains. This chapter explores the theoretical foundations and potential applications of this emerging technology.

Introduction to the Concept of Nano Networks

Nano networks consist of interconnected devices at the nanometer scale, typically ranging from 1 to 100 nanometers. These networks represent the theoretical extension of communication capabilities to the smallest possible scales, potentially enabling new forms of sensing, actuation, and computation.

Key Characteristics of Nano Networks Include

- **Extreme miniaturization**: Components operate at molecular or atomic scales.
- **Bio-inspired design**: Many concepts draw from biological systems like cellular communication.
- **Novel communication methods**: Traditional electromagnetic communication may be replaced by molecular, acoustic, or quantum approaches.
- **Ultra-low power operation**: Energy constraints are even more severe than in conventional IoT devices.

The theoretical foundation for nano networks comes from advances in nanotechnology, particularly the development of nano-scale components such as molecular transistors, nano-sensors, and nano-actuators.

Potential Future Integration with IoT Ecosystems

The integration of nano networks with broader IoT ecosystems could create multi-scale sensing and communication capabilities:

- **Hierarchical architectures**: Nano networks could form the lowest tier of multi-level IoT systems, with data aggregated and relayed to larger devices.
- **Interface mechanisms**: Specialized gateway devices could translate between nano-scale communications and conventional protocols.
- **Domain-specific applications**: Initial integration might focus on specific domains like healthcare or materials monitoring.

This integration would bridge the gap between the macro-scale world of conventional IoT and the nano-scale world of molecular processes, enabling comprehensive monitoring and potentially control of phenomena across multiple scales.

Challenges and Research Directions for Nano-Scale Communication

The development of practical nano networks faces several significant challenges:

- **Communication mechanisms**: Establishing reliable communication channels between nano-devices.
- **Energy supply**: Powering nano-devices for extended periods.

- **Fabrication techniques**: Manufacturing functional devices at nano scale.
- **Coordination and control**: Managing the behavior of potentially billions of nano-devices.
- **Integration with macro systems**: Bridging between nano-scale and conventional networks.

Research directions addressing these challenges include:

- **Molecular communication**: Using chemical signals for information exchange, similar to biological cells.
- **Electromagnetic nano-communication**: Adapting traditional wireless techniques to nano-scale constraints.
- **Energy harvesting**: Capturing energy from ambient sources at the nano scale.
- **Self-organization**: Developing algorithms for autonomous coordination among nano-devices.

While nano networks remain largely theoretical at present, ongoing research in nanotechnology and communication systems may eventually enable their practical implementation, potentially revolutionizing the scope and capabilities of the Internet of Things.

4.7 PRINCIPLES FOR FI ARCHITECTURE

WiFi architecture is created to offer seamless, high-speed, and secure wireless communication. Principles of WiFi architecture center around effective network design, strong signal transmission, security, scalability, and optimized performance.

A properly designed WiFi network includes a variety of components such as access points (APs), wireless controllers, authentication servers, and the backend infrastructure that provides stable and scalable connectivity. The following are the main principles that define WiFi architecture:

Layered Network Design for Efficiency

WiFi design has a layered structure like the OSI model to provide organized communication and interoperability.

- **Physical Layer (PHY):** Specifies the transmission of data through radio waves, such as frequency bands (2.4 GHz, 5 GHz, 6 GHz), modulation schemes, and power.
- **Data Link Layer (MAC Layer):** Handles packet delivery, error detection, and media access control (MAC) protocols like Carrier Sense Multiple Access with Collision Avoidance (CSMA/CA).
- **Network Layer:** Facilitates correct routing and connectivity among devices, with support for IPv4/IPv6 and DHCP for IP address assignment.
- **Application Layer:** Provides support for services such as VoIP, streaming, and cloud-based applications to enable seamless use of user-oriented applications over WiFi.

This organization allows WiFi networks to effectively manage communication between various network layers without compromising on performance and compatibility.

Centralized and Distributed Architectures

WiFi networks can be implemented with centralized or distributed architectures based on the complexity and size of the deployment.

- **Centralized Architecture:** Employed in enterprise scenarios where APs are controlled by a WLC. The WLC provides optimized traffic routing, security policies, and AP-to-AP handoffs for smooth connectivity.
- **Distributed Architecture:** In home and small office networks, independent access points are self-contained, performing routing, security, and quality of service (QoS) locally. Mesh WiFi systems employ a hybrid solution where several APs dynamically optimize linkages.

Selecting the appropriate architecture is critical to achieving scalability, performance optimization, and network manageability.

Frequency Band Utilization and Channel Management

WiFi is implemented on multiple frequency bands, each with unique characteristics:

- **2.4 GHz:** Has greater range but is more likely to suffer from congestion as it has few non-overlapping channels (just three: 1, 6, and 11).
- **5 GHz:** Provides greater speeds with more non-overlapping channels to minimize interference.
- **6 GHz (WiFi 6E and WiFi 7):** Increases bandwidth available considerably, which reduces congestion in high-density locations.

Optimized channel management avoids interference, enhances performance, and lessens latency. Automatic channel selection, DFS (dynamic frequency selection), and channel bonding are some techniques that enhance bandwidth usage optimization.

Security and Authentication Framework

WiFi networks need to have strong security measures in place to guard against intrusions and cyberattacks. Key security concepts are:

- **Encryption Standards:** WPA3 (WiFi Protected Access 3) offers secure encryption, which supersedes old WEP and WPA2 protocols.
- **Authentication Mechanisms:** Networks implement authentication models like 802.1X with RADIUS servers for corporate security, where only legitimate users can connect.
- **MAC Address Filtering:** Permits the connection of specific devices, eliminating unauthorized connections.
- **Intrusion Detection and Prevention Systems (IDS/IPS):** Detects and prevents suspicious traffic like rogue access points or unauthorized network sniffing.

Secure security policies guarantee secure data transfer, blocking cyber-attacks like man-in-the-middle (MITM) attacks, eavesdropping, and unauthorized access.

Smooth Roaming and Handoff Processes

WiFi networks must provide seamless connectivity as users roam from one access point to another. This is facilitated by:

- **802.11r (Fast BSS Transition - FT):** Minimizes authentication lag while roaming, essential for VoIP and video conferencing.

- **802.11k (Neighbor Reports):** Facilitates devices' discovery of the optimal access point to which to hand over, enhancing the efficiency of handoff.
- **802.11v (Network-Assisted Roaming):** Allows the network to steer devices toward optimal APs based on signal quality and congestion.

These mobile additions are essential to enterprise networks, hospitals, and smart city facilities where users demand uninterrupted connectivity.

Traffic Prioritization Quality of Service (QoS)

WiFi networks support various categories of traffic that have varying requirements for latency and bandwidth. QoS processes enable prioritization of essential data streams to provide efficient performance.

- **Wi-Fi Multimedia (WMM):** Enforces traffic prioritization among four classes—voice, video, best effort, and background traffic.
- **Packet Scheduling:** Provides preferential bandwidth to high-priority applications (e.g., video calls, gaming) over lower-priority applications (e.g., file downloads).
- **Bandwidth Allocation:** Restricts bandwidth for specific applications or users to avoid network congestion.

Through QoS, WiFi networks ensure performance for mission-critical applications, VoIP, and real-time streaming.

Scalability and Mesh Networking

WiFi architecture needs to be scalable to handle a growing number of devices and users.

- **Mesh Networking:** A self-healing network in which several APs collaborate to provide coverage without seams. Mesh networks automatically reroute traffic to the highest-performing node, with no dead spots.
- **Hierarchical Network Design:** Employs core, distribution, and access layers to maximize traffic distribution in large deployments (e.g., airports, stadiums).
- **Automatic Load Balancing:** Balances devices across available APs to avoid overload and optimize efficiency.

Scalable designs keep WiFi networks running reliably even as device density increases.

Self-Healing and Network Monitoring Capabilities

WiFi networks are required to be monitored and fine-tuned around the clock for reliability and performance.

- **AI-Powered Network Analysis:** Traffic behavior is studied and congestion anticipated using machine learning, which tunes network parameters accordingly.
- **Self-Healing Capabilities:** Power levels can be altered automatically, traffic can be routed around automatically, or even individual APs reboot automatically if anything goes wrong.
- **Remote Control & Cloud-Based Management:** Systems like Cisco Meraki and Aruba Central enable admins to centrally manage and configure WiFi networks remotely.

These guidelines provide minimum downtime and proactive problem-solving, increasing network stability in general.

Power Efficiency and Energy Management

WiFi networks need to maximize power efficiency, particularly for battery-operated IoT devices and mobile clients.

- **Target Wake Time (TWT - WiFi 6 feature):** Enables devices to plan ahead for their communication periods, minimizing power consumption in low-power devices such as smart sensors.
- **Beamforming:** Focuses WiFi signals on the associated devices, increasing efficiency and minimizing wasted transmission energy.
- **Smart AP Sleep Modes:** Access points scale power consumption by network demand, minimizing energy usage off-peak.

Low Energy WiFi architecture is critical for smart home, industrial IoT, and mass deployment.

Future of WiFi Architecture

With wireless technology advancing at breakneck pace, WiFi architecture continues to change:

- **WiFi 7 (802.11be):** Offers 320 MHz channel width, Multi-Link Operation (MLO), and lower latency, greatly increasing ease of use.
- **Integration with 5G:** Hybrid WiFi-5G networks will provide seamless connectivity, especially for enterprise and smart city applications.
- **AI-Driven Network Optimization:** Predictive AI will dynamically adjust WiFi parameters, ensuring optimal performance and security.

These innovations will further enhance WiFi's reliability, scalability, and user experience.

4.8 PHYSICAL LAYER AWARE NETWORK ARCHITECTURE FOR ENERGY EFFICIENCY

Energy efficiency remains one of the most critical challenges in IoT systems, particularly for battery-powered or energy-harvesting devices. Physical layer aware network architectures aim to optimize energy usage by considering the fundamental characteristics of wireless communication and hardware constraints in the design of network protocols and systems.

Optimizing the Physical Layer for Energy Conservation

The physical layer represents the foundation of wireless communication and offers significant opportunities for energy optimization:

- **Modulation schemes**: Selecting energy-efficient modulation approaches based on channel conditions and required data rates.
- **Transmission power control**: Adjusting output power to the minimum required for reliable communication.
- **Spectrum utilization**: Efficient use of available bandwidth to maximize data transfer per unit energy.
- **Error coding**: Balancing error correction capabilities with computational overhead.

Optimizations at this layer directly impact the energy required for successful data transmission, which often represents the largest energy expenditure in wireless sensor nodes.

Energy-Efficient Reconfigurable Antennas for Ultra-Low Power IoT Devices

Antenna design represents an often-overlooked aspect of energy efficiency in IoT devices:

- **Reconfigurable antennas**: Dynamically adjustable antennas that can modify their radiation patterns, polarization, or frequency response.
- **Directional transmission**: Focusing energy in the direction of the intended receiver rather than broadcasting omnidirectionally.
- **Adaptive matching**: Ensuring optimal power transfer between the radio and antenna under varying conditions.
- **Multi-band operation**: Supporting multiple frequency bands without requiring separate antenna systems.

Advanced antenna technologies can significantly reduce the energy required for successful communication, particularly in challenging environments with interference or obstacles.

Power Management Strategies for Energy Harvesting IoT Devices

Energy harvesting offers a path to perpetual operation for IoT devices, but requires sophisticated power management:

- **Harvest-aware operation**: Adapting device activity based on available and anticipated energy.
- **Energy storage optimization**: Efficient charging and discharging of energy storage elements.
- **Task scheduling**: Prioritizing activities based on energy availability and application requirements.
- **Adaptive duty cycling**: Adjusting active/sleep cycles to match energy availability.

These strategies enable devices to operate reliably even with unpredictable or intermittent energy sources, maximizing their functional availability while avoiding energy depletion.

Impact of Wireless Communication Technologies on Energy Consumption

Different wireless technologies offer varying trade-offs in terms of energy efficiency:

- **RFID**: Extremely low power requirements, but limited range and data rates.
- **Bluetooth Low Energy (BLE)**: Optimized for energy efficiency in personal area networks.
- **Wi-Fi**: Higher power consumption but greater bandwidth, with low-power modes like 802.11ah.
- **ZigBee**: Designed for low-power mesh networking in personal area networks.
- **NFC**: Very short range but extremely low power consumption for proximity applications.

The selection of appropriate wireless technology depends on the specific requirements of the application, with energy considerations often playing a decisive role in this choice.

Designing Energy-Efficient Routing Algorithms That Consider Physical Layer Characteristics

Cross-layer routing algorithms that incorporate physical layer awareness can achieve greater energy efficiency:

- **Link quality integration**: Routing decisions based on actual physical layer performance rather than hop count alone.
- **Dynamic transmission power**: Adjusting power levels based on route characteristics.
- **Interference-aware routing**: Avoiding paths with high interference levels.
- **Energy-balanced routing**: Distributing communication load to avoid premature depletion of specific nodes.

These approaches extend the operational lifetime of the overall network by making routing decisions that account for the physical realities of wireless communication and device constraints.

The physical layer represents the foundation upon which all higher-layer protocols operate, and its careful optimization is essential for achieving the energy efficiency required for practical deployment of large-scale IoT systems.

By incorporating awareness of physical layer characteristics into network architectures, designers can create systems that balance functionality with long-term operational sustainability.

4.9 INFORMATION-CENTRIC NETWORKING (ICN) AND THE EMBEDDED INTERNET

Information-Centric Networking (ICN) represents a fundamental shift from the traditional host-centric internet architecture to one that emphasizes content and information. This paradigm has particular relevance for IoT and embedded internet systems that generate and consume vast amounts of distributed data.

Introduction to the Principles of Information-Centric Networking

ICN transforms the basic communication model of the internet from one focused on where data is located to one focused on what the data is:

- **Named data objects**: Content is addressed by what it is (its name or identifier) rather than where it is located.
- **In-network caching**: Network elements can store content to serve future requests, reducing latency and bandwidth usage.
- **Built-in security**: Content can be secured directly rather than securing the communication channels.
- **Native multicast**: Efficient distribution of content to multiple consumers through replication at optimal network points.
- **Mobility support**: Content naming removes the dependence on fixed endpoints, simplifying mobility management.

This approach departs significantly from the traditional IP-based model where communication is primarily between specific hosts identified by addresses.

Potential Advantages of ICN for Handling the Vast Data Generated by IoT Devices

ICN offers several advantages that align particularly well with IoT scenarios:

- **Reduced bandwidth consumption**: Caching frequently accessed data closer to consumers minimizes redundant transmissions.
- **Improved resilience**: Data can be retrieved from multiple sources, enhancing availability even when specific devices are unreachable.
- **Simplified device discovery**: Content-based addressing can simplify the process of finding relevant data sources.
- **Enhanced security**: Securing the content itself rather than the communication path offers protection even when data traverses untrusted networks.
- **Support for intermittent connectivity**: Delayed or disrupted communication is better handled in a content-centric model.

These advantages address several key challenges in IoT data management, particularly in scenarios involving large numbers of devices generating similar data that may be consumed by multiple applications.

Mechanisms for Efficient Data Retrieval and Dissemination

ICN implementations employ several mechanisms to enable efficient data management in distributed environments:

- **Interest-based routing**: Requests for named content are forwarded through the network until they reach a source or cache.
- **Strategic caching**: Content can be cached based on popularity, importance, or network topology considerations.
- **Name-based aggregation**: Similar requests can be aggregated to reduce network load.
- **Pub-sub mechanisms**: Publishers can push data to interested subscribers without explicit requests.
- **Time-based relevance**: Content names can incorporate temporal aspects to manage freshness and validity periods.

These mechanisms create an infrastructure well-suited to the data-centric nature of many IoT applications, where the identity of specific data sources may be less important than the content they provide.

While ICN remains an evolving research area, its principles offer promising approaches to addressing the data management challenges inherent in large-scale IoT deployments. The alignment between ICN's content-centric philosophy and the data-driven nature of IoT suggests potential synergies that could shape the future evolution of the embedded internet.

4.10 STREAMING OF SCALABLE VIDEO OVER FI

Streaming video on WiFi poses a number of challenges such as network congestion, differences in device capabilities, and differences in bandwidth. To overcome these challenges, current streaming systems utilize scalable video streaming methods that adapt video quality dynamically depending on network status and device capability. Technologies such as adaptive bitrate streaming (ABR), sophisticated video codecs, WiFi 6 improvements, edge caching, and Quality of Service (QoS) optimization assist smooth and efficient video delivery on wireless networks.

Adaptive Bitrate Streaming (ABR) for Dynamic Quality Adjustment

One of the key methods for scalable video streaming is Adaptive Bitrate Streaming (ABR). ABR enables video quality to change dynamically in real-time according to the available bandwidth and network of the user.

- When network conditions are good, the streaming service provides high-definition video (e.g., 1080p or 4K).
- In case of congestion, the video stream is automatically downscaled to a lower resolution (e.g., 720p or 480p) to avoid buffering.
- This guarantees uninterrupted experience free from abrupt pause or lag.

Typical protocols supporting ABR are HLS (HTTP Live Streaming), MPEG-DASH, and Smooth Streaming. These protocols divide video into minute segments so that the player can choose the highest quality for each segment instead of streaming at a predetermined resolution.

Advanced Video Codecs for Bandwidth Efficiency

To save bandwidth while preserving high-quality images, new streaming services employ sophisticated video compression.

- **H.265/HEVC (High-Efficiency Video Coding):** Cuts file size by as much as 50% over H.264, supporting more efficient high-definition streaming.
- **AV1 Codec:** A royalty-free next-gen codec intended for even greater compression efficiency, cutting bandwidth use without sacrificing quality.
- **VP9 Codec:** Utilized by platforms such as YouTube for optimized streaming, especially at lower bitrates.

Through the use of these codecs, streaming websites provide seamless playback over WiFi connections even where multiple devices are online.

WiFi 6 and WiFi 6E Improvements to Video Streaming

WiFi 6 and WiFi 6E bring some improvements that improve video streaming performance.

- **OFDMA (Orthogonal Frequency-Division Multiple Access):** Effectively splits WiFi channels, minimizing latency and maximizing performance with multiple devices streaming at the same time.
- **MU-MIMO (Multi-User, Multiple Input, Multiple Output):** Enables routers to talk to more than one device simultaneously, minimizing bottlenecks and maximizing overall throughput.
- **Target Wake Time (TWT):** Maximizes battery life for battery-powered streaming devices such as smart TVs, smartphones, and tablets.
- **6 GHz Band in WiFi 6E:** Increases usable bandwidth, diminishing congestion and stream performance in packed networks.

Such advancements guarantee streams remain uninterrupted in highly populated areas with numerous connected devices.

Edge Caching and Content Delivery Networks (CDNs)

Edge caching and CDNs are employed by streaming providers to ensure diminished latency and better video stream performance.

- CDNs (Content Delivery Networks) cache copies of video content in various locations across the globe, so users get streams from the nearest server, minimizing buffering time.
- Edge caching caches commonly accessed content on local network nodes, enhancing access speed and minimizing unnecessary data transmission over WiFi.

For instance, Netflix's Open Connect CDN distributes content in an efficient manner by storing popular titles near the users, offloading the traffic from internet service providers (ISPs) and enhancing playback quality.

QoS and Traffic Prioritization for Smooth Streaming

Routers use Quality of Service (QoS) and traffic prioritization mechanisms to provide uninterrupted video streaming.

- **Packet Prioritization:** Routers prioritize video streaming traffic above less important data, e.g., background downloads.
- **Dynamic Bandwidth Allocation:** Intelligent routers dynamically distribute bandwidth according to usage, guaranteeing that video streaming takes priority over less critical operations such as email or file downloading.
- **DSCP (Differentiated Services Code Point) Tagging:** Tagging and giving priority to video packets enhances the stability of streams.

QoS settings can also be configured on routers by users to provide a greater priority to streaming services to maintain a seamless experience even with several devices sharing the same network.

Low-Latency Streaming for Real-Time Applications

For live video applications such as live sports, video conferencing, and game streams, low-latency streaming is crucial.

- Low-Latency HLS (LL-HLS) and Low-Latency DASH minimize video buffering delay to achieve near-instant playback.
- WebRTC (Real-Time Communication Protocol) is employed for ultra-low-latency streaming in apps such as Zoom, Google Meet, and live interactive broadcasts.
- 5G and WiFi Convergence: Certain streaming services leverage hybrid 5G and WiFi technologies to provide a consistent connection in mobility scenarios (e.g., streaming on mobile devices when switching between WiFi and cellular connectivity).

These optimizations guarantee that real-time content is smooth and responsive, especially in competitive gaming and live event streaming applications.

AI-Based Video Streaming Improvements

Artificial intelligence (AI) is being increasingly used in video streaming workflows to improve quality and efficiency.

- **AI-Driven Upscaling:** Technologies such as NVIDIA's AI-driven upscaling enhance video resolution in real-time, so lower-quality streams look higher-resolution.

- **Content-Aware Encoding:** AI dynamically adapts compression rates according to the complexity of scenes, ensuring efficient bandwidth usage without sacrificing quality.
- **Predictive Buffering:** AI examines network patterns and user behavior to pre buffer video segments ahead of time, minimizing playback delays.

By adding AI-based methods, streaming services can enhance video quality even further while reducing data usage on WiFi networks.

Video Streaming Over WiFi Challenges and Future Directions

Video streaming over WiFi, although greatly improved, continues to have issues like network congestion, interference, and signal loss. Future developments will further enhance scalability and reliability:

- **WiFi 7:** Will likely add 320 MHz channel width, enhanced MU-MIMO, and better OFDMA for further improved video streaming quality.
- **Edge Computing:** Video streaming platforms will use local edge servers to render and deliver video streams with less latency.
- **AI-Driven Network Optimization:** AI-based routers will forecast and dynamically adjust network conditions in real-time, further eliminating buffering and lag.

4.11 MEDIA SEARCH AND RETRIEVAL IN FI

With the accelerated development of digital media, effective search and retrieval processes over WiFi networks have become crucial to ensure seamless user experience. Media search and retrieval are the processes of searching, indexing, and retrieving multimedia content like video, images, and audio files over a wireless network. An optimally designed system guarantees quick, secure, and correct retrieval of media without congesting the network. Several methods, such as AI-based indexing, peer-to-peer sharing, predictive query processing, and caching, improve the effectiveness of media retrieval.

AI-Driven Content Indexing and Metadata Extraction

For quick searches, WiFi systems utilize artificial intelligence (AI) and machine learning (ML) to scan media files and extract metadata. AI-driven content indexing enables media files to be indexed based on characteristics such as title, description, file type, timestamps, and even visual or audio identification. For example, a home system with a media server can automatically label video files according to detected faces, objects, or speech transcripts. The intelligent labeling enhances search effectiveness, allowing users to locate particular media content easily via keywords, voice commands, or filters.

Peer-to-Peer (P2P) Media Sharing Over WiFi

One of the main benefits of using WiFi-based media retrieval is that media can be transferred and accessed directly between devices without the need for the internet. Peer-to-peer (P2P) sharing of media, facilitated by WiFi Direct or local network file-sharing protocols, makes it possible for users to access media from other devices that are part of the same WiFi network. For instance, at home, members of the household can access a common media library saved in a home server or any other appliance without having to use cloud services. This method not only accelerates file access but also saves bandwidth as data does not have to be uploaded or downloaded from the internet.

Predictive Search and Efficient Query Handling

Media search on WiFi incorporates sophisticated query processing capabilities to enhance the user experience. Predictive search functionality taps into historic user activity and machine learning algorithms to offer media suggestions based on past behavior even before a complete search query is initiated. For instance, if a user tends to watch a specific type of films, related content can be elevated in search rankings. In addition, voice search enables users to access media through natural language processing (NLP), which makes content discovery more natural.

Content Caching and Pre-Fetching for Accelerated Retrieval

To minimize latency and enhance media access speeds, WiFi networks utilize caching and pre-fetching techniques. Media files that are accessed most often are cached locally so that they can be accessed instantly without further network load. For instance, within a business environment, the training video accessed by several workers may be buffered in the local WiFi network in order to avoid repetitive streaming via the internet. Pre-fetch mechanisms track user trends and download, or buffer media intended to be opened soon automatically in order to minimize latency even where the bandwidth is low.

Role-Based Access Control and Security in Media Retrieval

Security is an important feature in media search and retrieval via WiFi because improper access to personal content opens up chances of data breaches. Role-based access control (RBAC) techniques prevent unauthorized users from downloading particular media files. For example, a corporate network can impose access restrictions so that sensitive presentations are available to employees who possess the correct clearance level. Moreover, encryption methods, like WPA3 security and end-to-end encryption, ensure unauthorized interception of media streams is prevented. Digital Rights Management (DRM) may also be employed to limit copying or redistribution of protected material.

Cloud and Hybrid WiFi Media Retrieval Systems

Although local WiFi-based retrieval is effective, most systems incorporate cloud storage for scalable media access. Hybrid systems combine cloud storage with local caching to make sure that users can access media even when the local network has constraints. For instance, a smart home media system can keep high-definition movies in the cloud and frequently viewed titles in a local cache for instant access. Cloud synchronization ensures that media libraries are synchronized across multiple devices.

4.12 FI SELF-MANAGEMENT SCENARIOS

WiFi self-management is the capability of a wireless network to manage performance, security, and resource allocation automatically without the need for human intervention. Following are important scenarios where self-management is important, and how WiFi addresses each scenario.

Adaptive Channel Selection

Scenario

There are several WiFi routers in a dense apartment complex using overlapping channels that result in interference and delayed speeds.

How WiFi Handles It

Automatic Channel Scanning: WiFi routers regularly scan the airwaves to identify congestion and interference from neighboring networks.

- **Dynamic Channel Switching:** Routers switch automatically to the least congested channel (e.g., shifting from channel 6 to channel 11 in the 2.4 GHz band).
- **AI-Based Learning:** Newer WiFi systems employ machine learning to anticipate interference patterns and change channels ahead of time before congestion sets in.
- **Dual-Band & Tri-Band Switching:** When interference is sensed on 2.4 GHz, the system can move devices to the 5 GHz or 6 GHz band for enhanced performance.

Band Steering

Scenario

A user's device is joined to the 2.4 GHz band rather than 5 GHz, even when in close proximity to the router, causing unnecessary congestion and reduced speeds.

How WiFi Solves It

- **Device Recognition:** Routers recognize dual-band-capable devices and push them to the 5 GHz band where feasible.
- **Signal Strength Analysis:** If a device has a good signal in 5 GHz but associates with 2.4 GHz, the router forces reassociation with the higher band.
- **Load Balancing:** If there are too many devices on 5 GHz, the router balances evenly across bands to ensure optimal speeds.

Power and Coverage Optimization

Scenario

At the workplace, employees in one part of the building are stuck with weak WiFi, and unoccupied spaces enjoy great coverage.

How WiFi Fixes It

- **Dynamic Power Adjustment:** Routers enhance the power of transmissions in weak signal regions and minimize power consumption in underused regions in order to conserve energy.
- **Beamforming Technology:** Beamforming by WiFi 6 routers channels signals towards the devices it connects rather than transmitting signals in all directions.
- **Mesh Network Optimization:** Nodes in mesh WiFi systems power-level and reposition themselves dynamically to remove dead spots.

Automatic Security Patching

Scenario

A user's router has aged firmware installed, making it susceptible to cyber-attack in the form of unauthorized access and malware infection.

How WiFi Solves It

- **Automatic Firmware Updates:** Routers automatically scan for updated firmware and install it without any intervention.
- **Threat Detection & Response:** AI-driven security systems scan traffic for anomalies, like unauthorized login attempts, and respond (e.g., blocking suspicious devices).
- **Self-Healing Security:** If a vulnerability is attacked, new WiFi systems can quarantine infected devices and block network-wide breaches.

Quality of Service (QoS) Optimization

Scenario

A home has several devices streaming video, playing online games, and video calling at the same time, leading to network congestion and lag.

How WiFi Solves It

- **Application-Based Prioritization:** WiFi infrastructure gives priority to bandwidth for latency-critical applications such as video conferencing and gaming against background downloads.
- **Packet Shaping:** Routers handle data packets by QoS rules to provide priority to latency-sensitive applications.
- **MU-MIMO & OFDMA:** WiFi 6 applies Multi-User MIMO and Orthogonal Frequency-Division Multiple Access (OFDMA) for efficient handling of multiple devices without network slowdown.

Smart Roaming & Seamless Handoff

Scenario

A user navigates through a big house or office, leading to constant disconnections as their device roams between access points.

How WiFi Manages It

- **802.11r Fast Roaming:** Devices pre-authenticate with several access points beforehand, minimizing handoff time when roaming between them.
- **802.11k Neighbor Reports:** WiFi clients are given a list of the best available access points in the vicinity and switch over automatically.
- **802.11v Network-Assisted Roaming:** Access points actively direct devices to the optimal connection choice based on signal quality and load

AI-Powered Network Diagnostics & Self-Healing

Scenario

A user is getting slow internet speed but has no idea if it's due to their ISP, network overload, or device issues.

How WiFi Solves It

- **Automatic Speed Tests:** The router is continuously performing speed tests and identifying anomalies in ISP performance.
- **Network Congestion Notifications:** AI inspects busy time periods and recommends off-peak times for bandwidth-intensive operations.
- **Self-Healing Techniques:** The router self-reboots, remaps IP addresses, or applies corrections when network instability is found.

SUMMARY

Technologies under Future Internet (FI) focus on increasing the connectivity, efficiency, and intelligence of networks. Mobile crowd sensing uses the real-time data capture capabilities of a large number of user's device for the purposes of smart applications. The wireless protocol stack serves the embedded systems architecture together with WSNs and the Internet of Things (IoT) devices. With M2M communication and the embedded internet, devices can communicate with each other autonomously, and nano networks further extend the IoT to the world of the very small. Principles of FI architecture design call for flexibility and adaptability, which is provided by a network architecture that is aware of the physical layer and guarantees communication through data delivery. The process of Information Centric Networking (ICN) shifts from the use of a host as a source of communication address to the source of information which enables the increasing efficiency in the content delivery. Streaming scalable video in FI enables the delivery of dynamic content improving media retrieval. Scenarios directed toward self-management in FI utilize a high level of automation and AI-based decision-making in order to improve network reliability and performance. All these functions integrate logically in the evolution of next co-working networks and intelligent digital ecosystems.

5

UNIT

Application Environment

5.1 INTRODUCTION TO APPLICATION ENVIRONMENTS IN MMBD-IOT

The convergence of Multimedia Big Data (MMBD) and the Internet of Things (IoT) represents one of the most significant technological paradigms shifts of the modern era. This fusion creates complex ecosystems where massive amounts of multimedia data are continuously generated, processed, and analyzed to drive intelligent decision-making across numerous sectors.

The Convergence of MMBD and IoT

IoT has emerged as one of the most prolific generators of multimedia big data in today's digital landscape. With billions of interconnected devices deployed globally—from environmental sensors and surveillance cameras to wearables and industrial equipment—the IoT ecosystem produces an unprecedented volume of diverse multimedia content. This data includes images, videos, audio recordings, time-series sensor readings, and complex multi-modal information streams.

What distinguishes MMBD in IoT environments is not merely its volume but its heterogeneity, velocity, and complexity. Unlike traditional structured data, multimedia content from IoT devices presents unique challenges:

- **Heterogeneity**: Data comes in widely varying formats, resolutions, and modalities
- **Velocity**: Real-time or near-real-time generation requiring immediate processing
- **Veracity**: Varying degrees of quality and reliability from diverse sources
- **Value extraction**: Requiring specialized analytics to derive actionable insights

These characteristics necessitate specialized computing approaches that can efficiently capture, transmit, store, process, and analyze MMBD in IoT contexts while addressing constraints related to bandwidth, energy consumption, security, and privacy.

Overview of Application Areas

1. **Precision Agriculture**: Leveraging multimedia data from various sensors to optimize crop production, monitor plant health, and enable sustainable farming practices.
2. **Network-Based Applications**: Examining how network infrastructures support MMBD in IoT across supply chains, transportation, healthcare, and disaster management.
3. **Video Communication Technologies**: Investigating protocols and standards facilitating real-time video communication in IoT ecosystems.

4. **Case Studies**: Analyzing specific implementations in military surveillance, interactive TV, video-on-demand services, and smart phone applications.

Each of these domains presents unique challenges and opportunities for MMBD computing in IoT environments, requiring tailored approaches to address their specific requirements.

5.2 RECENT ADVANCEMENTS IN MMBD COMPUTING FOR IOT IN PRECISION AGRICULTURE

The agricultural sector has undergone a profound digital transformation in recent years, with precision agriculture emerging as a prominent application environment for MMBD-IoT technologies. This revolution is fundamentally changing how farmers monitor crops, manage resources, and make decisions.

The Digital Revolution in Agriculture and the Rise of MMBD

The proliferation of affordable electronic devices has catalyzed massive data acquisition in agriculture from diverse sources. Modern farms are increasingly equipped with:

- Weather stations collecting environmental parameters
- Soil moisture sensors providing real-time hydration data
- Drones capturing high-resolution aerial imagery
- Multispectral and hyperspectral cameras monitoring plant health
- GPS-enabled equipment recording precise location data

This data explosion presents both opportunities and challenges. The overwhelming quantity of multimedia data makes traditional storage, transmission, and analysis methods inadequate. However, effective utilization of this MMBD offers unprecedented insights into agricultural operations, enabling data-driven decision support systems that can optimize yields, reduce resource usage, and enhance sustainability.

Cyber-Physical Systems (CPS) for Smart Farming

Precision agriculture increasingly relies on Cyber-Physical Systems that integrate physical elements with computational components. These systems create a seamless bridge between the physical world of crops, soil, and weather and the digital realm of data analytics and decision support.

CPS in agriculture typically involves:

- **Sensing layer:** Physical sensors capturing environmental parameters and multimedia data
- **Communication layer**: Wireless networks transmitting data to processing centers
- **Computation layer**: Analytics platforms processing multimedia data
- **Control layer**: Automated or semi-automated systems implementing decisions

This integration enables real-time sensing and dynamic control using computation, communications, and control (3C) technology. For example, irrigation systems can automatically adjust water delivery based on soil moisture sensor readings and weather forecasts, optimizing water usage while maintaining ideal growing conditions.

Multimedia Data Collection Approaches in Precision Agriculture

Modern precision agriculture employs various approaches to collect diverse multimedia data:

IoT Sensors

IoT sensor networks monitor crucial environmental parameters including:

- Temperature and humidity
- Atmospheric pressure
- CO_2 and other gas concentrations
- Soil moisture and composition
- Light intensity and spectrum

These sensors often form wireless mesh networks in agricultural fields, providing continuous data streams that can be correlated with crop performance metrics.

Imaging and Remote Sensing

Various imaging technologies play a critical role in monitoring plant health and development:

- **Digital RGB cameras**: For visual inspection and growth monitoring
- **Infrared (IR) cameras**: Detecting heat signatures and stress indicators
- **Multispectral cameras**: Measuring reflected light in specific wavelength bands
- **Hyperspectral imaging**: Providing detailed spectral information across hundreds of bands

These imaging systems can be deployed on various platforms:

- Ground-based stationary systems
- Mobile platforms (tractors, rovers)
- Aerial systems (drones, aircraft)
- Satellite-based remote sensing

Wireless Communication Technologies

Data transmission in agricultural environments typically leverages:

- **ZigBee**: Low-power, short-range communication suitable for sensor networks
- **WiFi**: Higher bandwidth connections for transmitting images and video
- **RFID**: Tracking physical assets and livestock
- **LoRaWAN and NB-IoT**: Long-range, low-power communication for remote areas
- **5G**: Emerging high-bandwidth, low-latency connectivity for real-time applications

Opportunities and Challenges

The integration of MMBD-IoT in precision agriculture offers significant opportunities:

- **Yield optimization** through early detection of plant stress and disease
- **Resource efficiency** via precise application of water, fertilizers, and pesticides

- **Sustainability improvements** through reduced environmental impact
- **Labor optimization** with targeted interventions instead of blanket treatments
- **Predictive insights** leveraging historical data and machine learning

However, substantial challenges remain:

- **Data heterogeneity**: Integrating diverse data types and formats
- **Unstructured nature**: Extracting meaningful insights from complex multimedia content
- **Storage and processing**: Managing massive volumes of data with limited infrastructure
- **Standardization**: Lack of common protocols and formats across devices and platforms
- **Connectivity**: Limited bandwidth and reliability in rural agricultural areas
- **Energy constraints**: Powering distributed sensors in remote locations

Addressing these challenges requires innovative approaches to MMBD computing specifically tailored to agricultural environments.

5.3 NETWORK-BASED APPLICATIONS OF MMBD COMPUTING IN IOT ENVIRONMENT

Network infrastructure forms the critical backbone for MMBD-IoT applications across numerous sectors. The effective management and utilization of network resources are essential for the success of applications generating and consuming multimedia big data.

The Role of Smart Devices and Innovative Technologies

Modern business management increasingly relies on internet-connected devices that form the foundation of IoT ecosystems. These smart devices range from simple sensors to sophisticated multimedia equipment, all generating data that flows through various connecting mediums:

- **Wi-Fi:** High-bandwidth wireless connectivity for video and complex data
- **Bluetooth**: Short-range communication for personal area networks
- **Infrared**: Direct line-of-sight communication for specific applications
- **Cellular technologies**: Wide-area connectivity through 4G/5G networks
- **Hotspot technologies**: Ad-hoc network creation for temporary deployments

These connected devices typically transmit their data to centralized or distributed servers where sophisticated analysis occurs, enabling informed decision-making based on comprehensive data insights. The bidirectional nature of these connections allows not only data collection, but also remote control and configuration of devices based on analytical outcomes.

Application Areas

Network-based MMBD-IoT applications span numerous domains, each with unique requirements and characteristics:

Supply Chain Management

Supply chains leverage MMBD-IoT for:

- Real time inventory tracking through RFID and camera systems
- Quality monitoring via temperature and humidity sensors
- Location tracking through GPS and other positioning technologies
- Predictive maintenance using vibration and acoustic sensors

These applications generate diverse multimedia data that must be efficiently transmitted, processed, and analyzed to optimize logistics operations and minimize disruptions.

Transportation

Smart transportation systems utilize:

- Traffic monitoring cameras
- Vehicle telemetry sensors
- Environmental monitoring stations
- Passenger counting systems
- Infrastructure condition sensors

The resulting multimedia data helps optimize traffic flow, reduce congestion, enhance safety, and improve the overall efficiency of transportation networks.

Healthcare

Healthcare applications include:

- Remote patient monitoring through wearable devices
- Medical imaging from portable diagnostic equipment
- Telemedicine video consultations
- Environmental monitoring in healthcare facilities
- Medication and equipment tracking

These applications often have stringent requirements for data quality, reliability, security, and privacy, necessitating specialized network architectures and protocols.

Environment and Disaster Management

Environmental monitoring and disaster response utilize:

- Weather stations and atmospheric sensors
- Flood and water level monitors
- Seismic activity sensors
- Forest fire detection cameras
- Pollution monitoring equipment

The time-sensitive nature of disaster management applications places particular emphasis on network reliability and low-latency communication.

Smart Homes

Residential IoT applications incorporate:

- Security cameras and motion sensors

- Voice-controlled assistants
- Energy management systems
- Entertainment and media streaming
- Automated appliances and systems

These applications often generate significant multimedia content that must be efficiently processed and analyzed within the limited network infrastructure of residential environments.

Smart Farming

As explored in Chapter 2, agricultural applications leverage:

- Field sensors for environmental monitoring
- Imaging systems for crop health assessment
- Automated irrigation and fertilization systems
- Livestock monitoring and management
- Harvest optimization technologies

IoT-Based Big Data Processing

The effective analysis and management of IoT-based multimedia big data are crucial for deriving business value. Organizations increasingly implement sophisticated data processing pipelines that:

1. **Collect** raw multimedia data from distributed IoT devices
2. **Pre-process** data to filter, normalize, and prepare it for analysis
3. **Store** processed data in appropriate databases or data lakes
4. **Analyze** using advanced techniques such as computer vision, machine learning, and time-series analysis
5. **Visualize** results through intuitive dashboards and reporting tools
6. **Act** on insights through automated systems or human decision-makers

This end-to-end processing enables organizations to make well-informed decisions based on comprehensive data insights, improving operational efficiency, enhancing customer experiences, and creating new business opportunities.

Network Architectures and Considerations for MMBD in IoT

Network architectures for MMBD-IoT applications typically follow a layered approach:

1. **Physical (Sensing) Layer**: Comprising the IoT devices that capture multimedia data
2. **Network Layer**: Responsible for data transmission using appropriate protocols
3. **Application Layer**: Where data processing, analysis, and visualization occur

Key considerations in designing these networks include:

- **Quality of Service (QoS)**: Ensuring sufficient bandwidth, low latency, and minimal packet loss for multimedia applications
- **Scalability**: Accommodating growing numbers of devices and increasing data volumes

- **Heterogeneity**: Supporting diverse device types and communication protocols
- **Energy efficiency**: Minimizing power consumption, especially for battery-operated devices
- **Security**: Protecting sensitive data and preventing unauthorized access
- **Reliability**: Ensuring consistent performance in varying environmental conditions
- **Edge computing**: Processing data closer to its source to reduce bandwidth requirements and latency

Addressing these considerations requires careful network planning and the selection of appropriate technologies and protocols tailored to the specific requirements of each application environment.

5.4 H.322 STANDARD AND ITS RELEVANCE

Communication standards play a critical role in enabling interoperability and ensuring quality of service in multimedia applications over networks. The H.322 standard represents an important framework in this domain, particularly for certain IoT application environments.

Introduction to the H.322 Standard

H.322 is a telecommunication standard developed by the International Telecommunication Union (ITU) that specifies protocols for audiovisual communication sessions over guaranteed quality of service packet networks. As an extension of the more widely known H.323 family of standards, H.322 addresses specific requirements for multimedia communication in environments where certain network performance parameters can be guaranteed.

Key features of the H.322 standard include:

- Support for real-time audio and video transmission
- Mechanisms for session establishment and termination
- Protocols for negotiating media capabilities
- Methods for synchronizing multimedia streams
- Error recovery and resilience techniques
- Quality of service management
- Integration with existing network infrastructures

H.322 implements a connection-oriented approach, establishing dedicated virtual circuits for multimedia sessions to ensure consistent performance and reliability.

Relevance of Connection-Oriented Protocols in IoT Applications

While many modern IoT applications leverage connectionless protocols like UDP for their efficiency and lower overhead, connection-oriented approaches like those specified in H.322 remain valuable in specific scenarios:

Mission-Critical Applications

In applications where reliability and guaranteed delivery are paramount—such as remote healthcare monitoring, industrial control systems, or safety-critical infrastructure—connection-oriented protocols provide essential guarantees for multimedia data transmission.

Quality-Sensitive Multimedia

Applications requiring high-quality, uninterrupted multimedia streams benefit from the established circuits and quality guarantees provided by connection-oriented protocols. Examples include:

- Telemedicine with diagnostic-quality video
- Remote surveillance for security applications
- Industrial inspection using high-resolution imagery
- Immersive virtual reality experiences

Considerations for Integrating H.322 with MMBD and IoT Environments

When implementing H.322 in MMBD-IoT applications, several factors must be considered:

Overhead and Efficiency

Connection-oriented protocols typically introduce additional overhead for connection establishment, maintenance, and termination. This overhead must be weighed against the benefits in each application context, particularly for resource-constrained IoT devices.

Scalability Challenges

Maintaining connection state for numerous devices can strain network infrastructure. Implementations must consider how to efficiently manage large numbers of concurrent connections in dense IoT deployments.

Heterogeneous Device Support

MMBD-IoT environments often include devices with varying capabilities. H.322 implementations must accommodate this diversity through flexible negotiation mechanisms and adaptive quality management.

Integration with Edge Computing

Distributing H.322 protocol handling across edge computing nodes can help address scalability challenges and reduce latency, particularly important for real-time multimedia applications.

The H.322 standard and similar connection-oriented approaches continue to provide value in specific MMBD-IoT application environments where reliability, quality, and deterministic performance are essential requirements.

5.5 PROTOCOL STACK AND CALL SETUP IN NETWORKED MULTIMEDIA SYSTEMS

Networked multimedia systems in IoT environments rely on sophisticated protocol stacks and call setup procedures to establish, maintain, and terminate multimedia sessions efficiently. Understanding these foundational elements is crucial for designing effective MMBD-IoT applications.

Protocol Stacks for Multimedia Communication

Multimedia communication in IoT environments typically employs layered protocol architectures that provide modular functionality and abstraction. These stacks generally align with the OSI or TCP/IP reference models, with adaptations specific to multimedia requirements.

Application Layer

The uppermost layer handles application-specific functions including:

- User interfaces and experience management
- Content encoding and decoding
- Media synchronization
- Session control and management
- Quality of experience monitoring

Common protocols at this layer include SIP (Session Initiation Protocol), RTSP (Real-Time Streaming Protocol), and application-specific APIs.

Presentation Layer

This layer addresses:

- Media format negotiation
- Compression and decompression
- Encryption and decryption
- Format translation between heterogeneous systems

Codecs like H.264/H.265 for video and AAC/Opus for audio operate at this layer.

Session Layer

Session management functionality includes:

- Establishing, maintaining, and terminating connections
- Session parameter negotiation
- Dialog management between endpoints
- Synchronization between multimedia streams

SIP and SDP (Session Description Protocol) are common protocols operating at this layer.

Transport Layer

Transport protocols provide:

- End-to-end delivery services
- Flow and congestion control
- Error detection and correction
- Segmentation and reassembly of data

RTP (Real-time Transport Protocol) running over UDP is commonly used for real-time multimedia, while TCP may be employed for reliable delivery of non-time-sensitive content.

Network Layer

This layer handles:

- Logical addressing (IP addressing)
- Routing between networks
- Traffic control and congestion management

IPv4 and IPv6 are the dominant protocols, with IPv6 increasingly important for IoT due to its expanded address space.

Data Link Layer

Link layer functionality includes:

- Physical addressing (MAC addressing)
- Media access control
- Error detection at the frame level

Ethernet, WiFi (IEEE 802.11), Bluetooth (IEEE 802.15.1), Zigbee (IEEE 802.15.4), and cellular standards operate at this layer.

Physical Layer

The lowest layer addresses:

- Transmission and reception of raw bit streams
- Definition of physical connectors and media
- Signal encoding and modulation
- Transmission rates and synchronization

Different physical media (wireless, optical, copper) have specific characteristics relevant to multimedia transmission.

Call Setup Procedures in Multimedia IoT

Establishing multimedia sessions in IoT environments involves several distinct phases:

Service Discovery

Before communication can begin, devices must:

- Discover available services and capabilities
- Identify potential communication partners
- Determine service characteristics and requirements

Discovery mechanisms include multicast DNS (mDNS), DNS-SD (Service Discovery), and application-specific discovery protocols.

Registration and Authentication

Secure multimedia communication requires:

- Device and user authentication
- Authorization verification
- Registration with control servers or directories
- Establishment of security contexts

These processes help prevent unauthorized access to sensitive multimedia streams and ensure proper resource allocation.

Session Establishment

The core call setup procedure includes:

- Initiating session requests
- Negotiating media parameters (codecs, formats, bit rates)
- Reserving necessary network resources
- Establishing media paths
- Synchronizing endpoints

Signaling protocols like SIP handle these functions, often working with other protocols like SDP for media description.

Media Exchange

Once the session is established:

- Media streams begin flowing between endpoints
- Quality of service monitoring commences
- Adaptation mechanisms respond to changing network conditions
- Synchronization is maintained between related streams

Session Modification

During active sessions, parameters may need adjustment:

- Adding or removing media streams
- Changing quality parameters in response to network conditions
- Transferring sessions between devices
- Adding participants (in multi-party scenarios)

Session Termination

Proper termination procedures ensure:

- Graceful release of resources
- Proper notification to all participants
- Accurate billing and accounting (where applicable)
- Updated status in registries and directories

5.6 CHALLENGES IN IOT MULTIMEDIA CALL SETUP

Adapting traditional call setup procedures to IoT environments presents several challenges:

Heterogeneity

IoT devices have widely varying capabilities, from simple sensors to sophisticated multimedia equipment. Call setup must accommodate this diversity through flexible negotiation mechanisms

Resource Constraints

Many IoT devices have limited processing power, memory, and energy. Lightweight protocols and efficient procedures are essential to minimize resource consumption.

Intermittent Connectivity

IoT devices may experience periodic disconnections or operate in challenging network environments. Call setup procedures must be resilient to these conditions, with appropriate recovery mechanisms.

5.7 SESSION INITIATION PROTOCOL (SIP) – COMPONENTS, MESSAGES, AND OPERATION

The Session Initiation Protocol (SIP) has emerged as a fundamental signaling protocol for establishing, modifying, and terminating multimedia sessions in networked environments. Its flexible, text-based architecture makes it particularly suitable for diverse IoT applications that involve multimedia communication.

Introduction to the Session Initiation Protocol

SIP is an application-layer control protocol designed for creating, modifying, and terminating sessions with one or more participants. These sessions may include internet calls, multimedia distribution, and multimedia conferences. SIP was developed by the Internet Engineering Task Force (IETF) and is defined in RFC 3261.

Key characteristics that make SIP valuable for MMBD-IoT applications include:

- **Text-based format:** Easy to debug and implement across diverse platforms
- **Extensibility**: Readily accommodates new features and capabilities
- **Modularity**: Works with various transport protocols and session types
- **Interoperability**: Functions alongside other protocols like RTP and SDP
- **Scalability**: Supports operation from simple point-to-point to complex enterprise deployments

SIP handles signaling aspects of communication sessions but does not transport the actual media content. Instead, it works in conjunction with protocols like RTP (Real-time Transport Protocol) for media delivery and SDP (Session Description Protocol) for media negotiation.

Key Components of a SIP Architecture

SIP networks typically comprise several functional elements:

User Agents (UAs)

User agents are the endpoints in SIP communication and come in two varieties:

- **User Agent Client (UAC)**: Initiates SIP requests
- **User Agent Server (UAS)**: Receives requests and returns responses

In IoT environments, user agents may include diverse devices such as:

- Smart cameras and surveillance systems
- Environmental sensor nodes with multimedia capabilities
- Industrial monitoring equipment
- Interactive displays and kiosks
- Wearable devices with audio/video capabilities

Proxy Servers

SIP proxy servers receive requests from UAs or other proxies and forward them towards the destination. They play crucial roles in:

- Request routing based on user location
- Policy enforcement for network usage
- Authentication and authorization
- Managing network traversal (NAT, firewalls)

In MMBD-IoT deployments, proxy servers often operate at the edge of networks, helping manage the transition between IoT domains and wider networks.

Registrars

Registrar servers accept REGISTER requests and maintain databases of user agents and their current locations. This function is essential in IoT environments where:

- Devices may have dynamic network addresses
- Users need to locate specific devices by logical identifiers
- Devices may connect through various access networks

Redirect Servers

Redirect servers receive SIP requests but instead of forwarding them, they respond with instructions directing the client to contact an alternate set of URIs. This capability supports:

- Load balancing across multiple servers
- Implementation of follow-me services
- Handling of device mobility scenarios

Back-to-Back User Agents (B2BUAs)

B2BUAs act as both a UAS and UAC, terminating incoming requests and generating outgoing requests. They provide greater control over session management and are used for:

- Protocol translation between incompatible endpoints
- Implementing complex services beyond basic proxying
- Enforcing security policies and media handling requirements

SIP Messages: Request and Response Types

SIP communication occurs through requests sent by clients and responses returned by servers. All messages use a text-based format similar to HTTP.

Request Methods

Core SIP request methods include:

- **INVITE:** Initiates a session or modifies parameters of an existing session
- **ACK**: Confirms reliable message exchanges
- **BYE**: Terminates an established session
- **CANCEL**: Cancels a pending request
- **REGISTER**: Registers user agent location
- **OPTIONS**: Queries the capabilities of servers

Extensions add methods like:

- **SUBSCRIBE/NOTIFY**: Implements event notification
- **MESSAGE**: Sends instant messages
- **INFO**: Communicates mid-session information
- **REFER**: Asks recipient to issue request to third party

Response Categories

SIP responses are grouped into six classes:

- **1xx (Provisional)**: Request received and being processed
- **2xx (Success)**: Request successfully received, understood, and accepted
- **3xx (Redirection)**: Further action needed to complete the request
- **4xx (Client Error)**: Request contains bad syntax or cannot be fulfilled by this server
- **5xx (Server Error)**: Server failed to fulfill an apparently valid request
- **6xx (Global Failure)**: Request cannot be fulfilled at any server

Message Structure

SIP messages consist of:

- **Start line**: Contains method or response code
- **Header fields**: Provide additional information about the message
- **Empty line**: Separates headers from message body
- **Message body** (optional): Often contains SDP for media description

Common headers include:

- **From and To:** Identify participants
- **Call-ID:** Uniquely identifies the session
- **Contact:** Provides direct route to participant
- **Content-Type:** Specifies type of message body
- **Via:** Records route taken by request

SIP Call Setup and Tear-down Operation

A typical SIP session follows several phases:

User Registration

Before receiving calls, user agents typically register their current location:

1. UA sends REGISTER request to registrar
2. Registrar authenticates the request
3. Registrar stores the binding between address-of-record and contact address
4. Registrar returns 200 OK response

Session Establishment

The basic call flow for establishing a session includes:

1. Caller UA sends INVITE containing SDP with media capabilities

2. Proxies route INVITE to callee UA
3. Callee UA returns 100 Trying response
4. Callee UA alerts user and sends 180 Ringing
5. When user answers, callee UA sends 200 OK with its own SDP
6. Caller UA acknowledges with ACK
7. Media session begins directly between endpoints

Session Modification

During an active session, parameters can be modified:

1. Either UA sends new INVITE (re-INVITE) with updated SDP
2. Other party responds with 200 OK and updated SDP
3. Original sender acknowledges with ACK
4. Media session continues with new parameters

Session Termination

To end a session:

1. Either UA sends BYE request
2. Other party responds with 200 OK
3. Media session terminates

Challenges and Adaptations

Implementing SIP in resource-constrained IoT environments requires consideration of:

- **Footprint optimization**: Minimizing code size for limited devices
- **Header compression**: Reducing bandwidth consumption
- **Energy efficiency**: Minimizing power usage during signaling
- **Simplified operation**: Adapting complex procedures for simple devices

5.8 SUPPORTING PROTOCOLS FOR SIP

While SIP provides robust signaling capabilities for multimedia sessions in IoT environments, it operates alongside several supporting protocols that handle complementary functions. Understanding these protocols and their interactions is essential for designing comprehensive MMBD-IoT communication solutions.

Media Gateway Access Protocol (MGCP)

MGCP is a protocol used for controlling media gateways from external call control elements called media gateway controllers or call agents. It complements SIP by providing fine-grained control over media handling components.

Role and Function

MGCP enables:

- Centralized call control architecture

- Detailed management of media streams
- Connection establishment between endpoints
- Event notification for media-related occurrences

Architecture Components

Key elements include:

- **Media Gateways (MGs):** Handle media conversion and transmission
- **Media Gateway Controllers (MGCs)**: Provide call control intelligence
- **Endpoints**: Logical entities that source or sink media streams
- **Connections**: Associations between endpoints for media transfer

Relevance to MMBD-IoT

In IoT environments, MGCP can be valuable for:

- **Heterogeneous Media Handling**: Managing conversion between different multimedia formats used by diverse IoT devices
- **Centralized Resource Management**: Optimizing utilization of network resources for multimedia transmission
- **Gateway Control**: Bridging between IoT multimedia domains and traditional telecommunications networks
- **Scalable Deployments**: Separating media handling from call control to support large-scale IoT implementations

Resource Reservation Protocol (RSVP)

RSVP is designed to reserve resources across a network to provide quality of service guarantees for application data streams, particularly important for multimedia applications.

RSVP provides:

- Path establishment for resource reservation
- Bandwidth allocation for specific traffic flows
- Prioritization of traffic based on QoS requirements
- Dynamic adaptation to changing network conditions

The RSVP process involves:

1. **Path Messages**: Sent from sender to receiver, establishing the route
2. **Resv Messages**: Sent from receiver to sender, requesting specific resources
3. **Confirmation**: Network devices along the path confirm resource availability
4. **Maintenance**: Periodic refresh messages maintain the reservation

RSVP in MMBD-IoT Applications

Resource reservation is particularly valuable in MMBD-IoT contexts for:

- **Mission-Critical Applications**: Ensuring reliable multimedia delivery for healthcare, safety, and security systems
- **Real-Time Monitoring**: Guaranteeing timely delivery of video and audio from monitoring devices
- **Industrial IoT**: Supporting deterministic networking requirements for industrial control and monitoring

- **Mixed-Criticality Networks**: Prioritizing essential multimedia traffic over less time-sensitive data

Session Description Protocol (SDP)

SDP provides a standard format for describing multimedia session parameters, enabling endpoints to agree on media characteristics before communication begins.
SDP descriptions contain three main sections:

- **Session-level information**: Includes session name, purpose, timing
- **Media-level information**: Specifies type, format, encoding, and transport
- **Connection information**: Provides network addresses and ports

Important SDP fields include:

- Media types (audio, video, application)
- Transport protocols (RTP/UDP/IP, TCP/IP)
- Media formats and codecs
- Bandwidth requirements
- Encryption keys and methods
- Media attributes for fine-tuning

SDP plays crucial roles in IoT multimedia applications:

- **Capability Negotiation**: Allowing heterogeneous devices to find compatible communication parameters
- **Resource Planning**: Providing information necessary for network resource allocation
- **Session Documentation**: Creating records of established sessions for monitoring and troubleshooting
- **Adaptation Support**: Facilitating changes to session parameters based on device and network conditions

Real-time Transport Protocol (RTP) and RTCP

RTP provides end-to-end delivery services for data with real-time characteristics, such as audio and video. Its companion protocol, RTCP (RTP Control Protocol), monitors quality of service and conveys information about participants.

RTP provides:

- Payload type identification
- Sequence numbering for loss detection
- Timestamping for synchronization
- Delivery monitoring
- Media-specific encoding support

RTCP includes several packet types:

- **Sender Reports (SR):** Transmission and reception statistics from active senders
- **Receiver Reports (RR):** Reception statistics from participants not actively sending
- **Source Description (SDES):** Source identification information
- Goodbye (BYE): Indicates end of participation
- **Application-specific (APP):** Custom extensions for specific applications

RTP and RTCP are essential for IoT multimedia applications:

- Enabling real-time delivery of sensor data, audio, and video
- Providing quality metrics for adaptive streaming decisions
- Supporting synchronization of multiple media streams
- Facilitating efficient multicast distribution for one-to-many scenarios

5.9 HARDWARE STANDARDS - SCIBUS AND S.100

Hardware standards and interfaces form the physical foundation of MMBD-IoT systems, determining how devices connect, communicate, and process multimedia data. Historical standards like Scibus and S.100 provide valuable insights into the evolution of hardware architectures, while modern interfaces address the specific requirements of contemporary IoT applications.

Introduction to Hardware Bus Standards

Scibus

Scibus (Scientific Computer Interface Bus) was developed as a standardized interface for connecting scientific instruments to computers. Key characteristics included:

- High-speed parallel data transfer
- Deterministic timing characteristics
- Support for multiple controllers and peripherals
- Standardized electrical and mechanical specifications
- Distance limitations of typically 20 meters

Historically, Scibus enabled the integration of diverse scientific equipment into unified measurement and control systems, laying groundwork for concepts now central to IoT sensor networks.

S.100 Bus

The S.100 bus architecture was a foundational standard for early microcomputer systems, providing:

- Modular expansion capabilities
- Standardized signal definitions
- Support for multiple processor architectures
- Electrical and mechanical compatibility between components
- Facilitating multi-vendor ecosystems

This standard enabled the development of extensible computer systems where capabilities could be added through standardized interface cards, conceptually similar to modern IoT systems where functionality is distributed across specialized devices.

Relevance of Hardware Standards in IoT Contexts

While specific historical standards like Scibus and S.100 are rarely used directly in modern IoT implementations, the principles they established continue to influence contemporary hardware architectures:

Hardware standards in IoT provide:

- Interoperability between devices from different manufacturers
- Reduced development costs through reusable components
- Simplified integration and deployment
- Longer lifecycle for deployed systems
- Enhanced reliability through proven designs

Modern IoT hardware standards adapt traditional concepts to address:

- Extreme power efficiency for battery-operated devices
- Miniaturization for unobtrusive deployment
- Wireless communication to eliminate physical connections
- Security hardening against physical and electronic attacks
- Environmental durability for deployment in harsh conditions

Contemporary IoT systems leverage various hardware interfaces optimized for multimedia data handling:

Sensor Interfaces

- **MIPI CSI (Camera Serial Interface)**: High-bandwidth interface for connecting camera sensors to processors
- **I^{2}S (Inter-IC Sound)**: Digital audio interface connecting audio codecs and processors
- **SPI (Serial Peripheral Interface)**: High-speed synchronous serial interface for sensors and memory
- **I^{2}C (Inter-Integrated Circuit)**: Low-speed bus for connecting multiple sensors to a single controller

Processing Interfaces

- **MIPI DSI (Display Serial Interface)**: High-speed interface for connecting displays to processors
- **PCIe (Peripheral Component Interconnect Express)**: High-bandwidth interface for connecting accelerators
- **AMBA (Advanced Microcontroller Bus Architecture)**: On-chip bus architecture for system-on-chip designs
- **AXI (Advanced eXtensible Interface)**: High-performance, flexible protocol for on-chip communication

Storage Interfaces

- **eMMC (embedded MultiMediaCard)**: Embedded storage for multimedia data
- **UFS (Universal Flash Storage)**: High-performance flash storage interface
- **NVMe (Non-Volatile Memory Express)**: Protocol for accessing high-speed storage over PCIe

Communication Interfaces

- **USB (Universal Serial Bus):** Versatile interface for device connectivity
- **Ethernet**: Standard for wired networking
- **HDMI (High-Definition Multimedia Interface)**: Audio/video interface for uncompressed data
- **Wi-Fi, Bluetooth, ZigBee, LoRa**: Wireless interfaces with varying characteristics

Role in MMBD Data Handling

Modern hardware interfaces play crucial roles in enabling efficient MMBD processing in IoT devices:

Data Acquisition

High-speed interfaces like MIPI CSI enable the capture of high-resolution video from camera sensors, while specialized audio interfaces facilitate high-quality sound acquisition. These interfaces must balance bandwidth with power consumption and physical size constraints.

Real-time Processing

On-chip bus architectures facilitate the movement of multimedia data between processing elements with minimal latency, enabling real-time analysis. Specialized accelerators for tasks like video encoding, computer vision, and machine learning connect through high-performance interfaces.

Storage and Retrieval

Modern storage interfaces support the high throughput required for multimedia data, allowing devices to buffer, cache, and archive content effectively. These interfaces increasingly incorporate features like command queuing and parallel operations to maximize performance.

Transmission

Communication interfaces determine how multimedia data moves between devices, with significant implications for bandwidth, latency, and reliability. The selection of appropriate interfaces depends on application requirements, environmental conditions, and deployment constraints.

The evolution from historical standards like Scibus and S.100 to modern specialized interfaces reflects the increasing sophistication of multimedia processing requirements in IoT environments, with contemporary systems balancing performance, power efficiency, and integration density to enable advanced applications.

5.10 CASE STUDY – VIDEO CONFERENCING IN IOT ENVIRONMENTS

Video conferencing represents a demanding MMBD-IoT application that illustrates many of the challenges and opportunities discussed in previous chapters. This case study examines how IoT technologies are transforming video communication systems and the unique considerations they present.

Iot-based Video Conferencing Faces Several Distinct Challenges

Many Iot Devices Operate With Limited Resources

- Restricted processing power for video encoding/decoding
- Limited memory for buffering and processing frames
- Constrained battery capacity affecting operational duration
- Reduced bandwidth compared to traditional networks

Iot Networks Typically Exhibit

- Fluctuating bandwidth availability
- Variable latency and jitter
- Occasional packet loss and connection drops
- Heterogeneous connection types with different characteristics

Video Conferencing Solutions Must Accommodate

- Varying camera resolutions and quality
- Different display capabilities (size, resolution, color depth)
- Diverse processing architectures (ARM, x86, specialized SoCs)
- Multiple operating systems and software environments

Iot Deployments May Involve

- Large numbers of concurrent video streams
- Geographically distributed participants
- Mixed device types participating in the same session
- Dynamic joining and leaving of participants

Addressing These Challenges Requires Specialized Approaches to Video Handling

Modern video conferencing in IoT leverages:

- Scalable Video Coding (SVC) to adapt resolution and frame rate to available bandwidth
- Hardware-accelerated encoding/decoding to minimize power consumption
- Ultra-low-latency codecs optimized for real-time communication
- Content-aware compression that preserves important visual elements

Techniques Include

- Region-of-interest encoding focusing bits on important areas (e.g., faces)
- Background subtraction and simplification
- Frame skipping during network congestion
- Parallel encoding of multiple quality levels for quick adaptation

To Handle Unstable Networks, Systems Implement

- Forward Error Correction (FEC) to recover from packet loss
- Intra-frame refreshes to prevent error propagation
- Multiple description coding for redundant transmission
- Prioritized packet retransmission focusing on visually significant data

Several architectural approaches have emerged to address the unique requirements of IoT video conferencing:

Cloud-Centric Architecture

This approach leverages cloud computing resources:

- IoT devices capture and transmit video to cloud servers
- Cloud performs transcoding, mixing, and distribution
- Minimal processing occurs on end devices
- Centralized management of sessions and resources

Advantages include scalability and consistent quality, while disadvantages include potential latency and privacy concerns.

Edge-Enhanced Architecture

Edge computing brings processing closer to devices:

- Edge nodes handle transcoding and adaptation
- Local traffic remains local, reducing backbone bandwidth
- Lower latency for time-sensitive interactions
- Graceful degradation during internet outages

This hybrid approach balances cloud scalability with edge responsiveness.

Mesh Architecture

Peer-to-peer communication can be effective for certain deployments:

- Direct device-to-device transmission where feasible
- Distributed mixing and forwarding of streams
- Reduced reliance on centralized infrastructure
- Adaptive topology based on network conditions

This approach can be particularly effective for local clusters of IoT devices.

Security and Privacy Considerations

IoT video conferencing presents unique security challenges:

Systems must implement:

- End-to-end encryption of video and audio streams
- Secure key exchange mechanisms
- Protected metadata and signaling
- Secure storage of recordings and session information

Robust mechanisms include

- Multi-factor authentication for sensitive sessions
- Device-level authentication and verification
- Fine-grained permissions for camera and microphone access
- Visual indicators when recording or streaming is active

Important features include

- Background blurring or replacement
- Visual and auditory notifications of active sessions
- Controls to limit camera field of view
- Options to disable persistent storage of communication

Real-world Implementation Example

An industrial IoT video conferencing system deployed in a manufacturing facility illustrates these concepts:

- Helmet-mounted cameras on maintenance personnel stream video to experts
- Edge servers in each facility handle initial processing and local distribution
- Adaptive bitrate adjusts to available bandwidth as workers move through the facility
- AI-enhanced video highlights potential issues and annotations overlay the video stream
- Recording integrates with maintenance databases for future reference and training
- End-to-end encryption protects proprietary manufacturing processes

This implementation demonstrates how IoT-based video conferencing can transform industrial operations through expert remote collaboration, reducing downtime and improving maintenance efficiency.

5.11 CASE STUDY – MILITARY SURVEILLANCE USING MMBD IN IoT

Military surveillance plays an essential role in national security, intelligence, and battlefield awareness. The assimilation of Massive Multimodal Big Data (MMBD) and the Internet of Things (IoT) has revolutionized classical military surveillance by facilitating real-time monitoring, decision-making, and threat identification. MMBD entails massive data acquisition from diverse sources such as satellites, drones, sensors, radars, and battlefield communication networks. The IoT ecosystem enables smooth connectivity among these devices so that battlefield operations are made intelligent with right and timely information.

MMBD's Role in Military IoT Monitoring

MMBD analyzes various data streams like images, videos, thermal imaging, audio, and sensor data to improve military intelligence. IoT technology like autonomous drones, robotic soldiers, smart wearable devices, and monitoring cameras all produce huge multimodal data volumes. Sophisticated Artificial Intelligence (AI) and Machine Learning (ML) algorithms process these datasets to identify anomalies, recognize threats, and forecast potential security threats. MMBD assists in integrating these multimodal inputs to develop an end-to-end situational awareness for military personnel and commanders.

Major Applications of MMBD in IoT-based Military Surveillance

- **Battlefield Monitoring:** IoT sensors and drones gather real-time information on enemy activity, terrain, and weather, enabling strategic decision-making.
- **Border Security:** IoT devices powered by MMBD scan border activity with thermal imaging, motion detection, and AI-driven intrusion detection systems.
- **Autonomous Combat Systems:** AI-powered unmanned ground and air vehicles (UGVs and UAVs) intensify surveillance and reconnaissance operations.
- **Cybersecurity & Signal Intelligence (SIGINT):** IoT-connected MMBD systems scan intercepted communications, cyber threats, and encrypted messages.
- **Disaster Response & Rescue Operations:** Military IoT sensors aid in search-and-rescue operations in natural disasters or combat operations.

Challenges and Security Concerns

Even though MMBD-based military IoT monitoring has many advantages, it encounters issues like information overload, cyber threats, jamming of signals, and lack of energy sources in isolated areas. Protection against sensitive military data requires encryption, blockchain, and AI-powered threat detection. Edge computing and fog computing are also used to locally process MMBD to limit latency and the reliance on central networks.

5.12 CASE STUDY - INTERACTIVE TV

The television industry is undergoing a significant transformation as it integrates IoT technologies and multimedia big data analytics to create more personalized, interactive, and immersive viewing experiences. This case study examines how these technologies are reshaping entertainment consumption.

Enhancing Television Interactivity through IoT

Traditional television has evolved from a passive, one-way medium to an interactive experience through IoT integration:

Connected Viewing Devices

The ecosystem now includes:

- Smart TVs with built-in connectivity and processing
- Set-top boxes and streaming devices
- Second-screen devices (smartphones, tablets)
- Smart speakers and voice assistants
- Ambient sensors monitoring viewing conditions
- Connected lighting and home automation systems

These devices communicate to create a synchronized, responsive viewing environment.

Interactive Capabilities

IoT enables novel interaction modalities:

- Voice control for content navigation and queries
- Gesture recognition for touchless control
- Biometric sensing for mood detection and content adaptation
- Cross-device synchronization for seamless viewing transitions
- Environmental adaptation (e.g., automatic lighting adjustment during viewing)
- Social viewing with remote participants

MMBD for Personalized Content and Recommendations

Multimedia big data analytics transform how content is discovered and consumed:

Complex User Profiling

Modern systems build sophisticated user models based on:

- Viewing history and patterns
- Content engagement metrics (completion rates, rewatching)
- Emotional responses detected through facial recognition
- Physiological reactions measured by wearables
- Cross-platform activity correlation
- Household composition and viewing group

Advanced Recommendation Engines

MMBD enables recommendation systems that consider:

Deep content analysis beyond simple genres and categories
Scene-level preferences rather than just show-level
Viewing context (time of day, device, location)
Mood-based matching using emotional analysis
Group recommendations for household viewing
Timing suggestions based on viewing availability patterns

Challenges in User Data Management and Privacy

The wealth of data collected creates significant privacy challenges:

Sensitive Data Collection

Interactive TV systems potentially gather:

- Viewing habits revealing personal interests and beliefs
- Voice recordings containing ambient household activity
- Camera feeds for gesture control and engagement measurement
- Presence information indicating home occupancy patterns
- Cross-correlation with other smart home data
- Social connections through shared viewing

Privacy Protection Mechanisms

- Effective systems implement:
- Transparent data collection policies with granular opt-in
- Local processing where possible to minimize data transmission
- Anonymization and aggregation of usage patterns
- Secure storage with encryption and access controls
- Automatic data aging and deletion policies
- User-accessible dashboards for privacy management

Regulatory Compliance

Solutions must address:

- Regional privacy regulations (GDPR, CCPA, etc.)
- Special protections for child viewers
- Consent management across household members
- Data portability and right-to-be-forgotten requirements
- Transparent AI decision-making explanations
- Cross-border data transfer restrictions

Integration with External Data Sources

Interactive TV increasingly incorporates data from beyond the viewing environment:

Social Media Integration

Connections with social platforms enable:

- Synchronized viewing with distant friends
- Content sharing and recommendations
- Real-time commentary and discussion
- Celebrity and creator interaction opportunities
- Community formation around specific content
- Influence measurement and trending content identification

Implementation Example: Next-Generation Entertainment Platform

A comprehensive interactive TV implementation leveraging MMBD-IoT might feature:

- Multi-room awareness with synchronized content following viewers
- Voice-controlled content discovery with natural conversation
- Emotion-detecting cameras that adjust content pacing to engagement
- Personalized audio mixing optimized for individual hearing profiles
- Second-screen experiences providing supplementary information
- Social co-viewing with distant friends appearing as virtual participants
- Content that adapts to ambient conditions (daylight, noise levels)
- Predictive caching based on viewing habits and schedule analysis

This evolution represents a fundamental shift from content delivery to experience creation, with MMBD-IoT technologies enabling unprecedented personalization and interactivity in home entertainment.

5.13 CASE STUDY - VIDEO ON DEMAND (VOD)

Video On Demand (VOD) services have transformed the entertainment sector by enabling customers to watch content at anytime, anywhere. Compared to traditional TV broadcasting, which is broadcast at a scheduled time, VOD sites allow customers to select from an extensive collection of movies, TV programs, and other video material on demand. Popular VOD services such as Netflix, Amazon Prime Video, Disney+, Hulu, and YouTube have transformed the way people consume media, leveraging high-speed internet, cloud computing, and artificial intelligence to enhance user experience.

VOD Business Models

VOD services operate under different business models, catering to various audience needs:

- Subscription Video On Demand (SVOD): Users pay a recurring fee for unlimited access to content (e.g., Netflix, Disney+).
- Transactional Video On Demand (TVOD): Paying per movie or episode, rental or buy (e.g., Apple iTunes, Google Play Movies).
- Ad-Supported Video On Demand (AVOD): Free with commercials (e.g., YouTube, Pluto TV).
- **Hybrid Models :** Platforms include free, ad-supported, and premium paid offerings (e.g., Hulu, Amazon Prime Video).
- **Case Example:** Netflix – A VOD Success Story

Netflix is one of the pioneers of VOD platforms, evolving from a DVD rental company in the early 2000s to a worldwide streaming behemoth. The business thrives on:

- **Content Strategy:** Creating original content such as Stranger Things, The Witcher, and Squid Game to appeal to an international audience.
- **AI-Powered Personalization:** Applying machine learning algorithms to offer content recommendations based on viewing history and user preferences.
- **Global Reach:** Crossing into global markets with localized content and multilingual subtitles.
- Cloud & CDN (Content Delivery Network): Utilizing AWS cloud services and distributed CDN servers to enable seamless streaming with reduced buffering.
- **Multi-Device Support:** Enabling seamless access across smartphones, smart TVs, tablets, gaming consoles, and web browsers.

Technological Advances in VOD

VOD platforms make use of advanced technologies to improve performance and user experience:

- **Adaptive Bitrate Streaming (ABR):** Provides seamless playback by dynamically adjusting video quality according to internet speed.
- **Artificial Intelligence (AI):** Enhances recommendation of content and improves search functionality.

- **5G & Edge Computing:** Minimizes latency and supports ultra-HD streaming on mobile.
- **Blockchain & Digital Rights Management (DRM):** Secures content against piracy and unauthorized sharing.

Challenges in VOD Industry

Even with its success, the VOD industry has a number of challenges:

- **Content Licensing Costs:** It is costly to acquire and produce high-quality content.
- Competition: The marketplace is filled with several players, and so there is subscriber churn.
- **Bandwidth & Streaming Quality:** It needs high-speed internet for a seamless experience, which is not always available across areas.
- **Piracy & Security Threats:** Piracy impacts revenue since unauthorized use of content reduces the same.
- **User Fatigue:** Consumers can be overwhelmed with too many subscription services.

Future Trends in VOD

The future of VOD will be led by:

- **AI-Generated Content Recommendations:** Smarter and more anticipatory analytics for personalized experiences.
- **Interactive & Immersive Content:** Augmentation of interactive narratives, AR/VR fusion, and 360-degree video.
- **Decentralized Streaming:** Blockchain-based video platforms to maximize transparency and revenue sharing for creators.
- **Expansion in Emerging Markets:** More localized content to address global diversity.

5.14 CASE STUDY – SMART PHONE

The fast growth of smartphones and the Internet of Things (IoT) has revolutionized contemporary life through improved connectivity, automation, and data sharing. Smartphones act as a focal point for IoT devices' control and monitoring, allowing smart home automation, healthcare monitoring, industrial uses, and real-time data analysis. This case study examines the use of smartphones in IoT, major applications, challenges, and prospects.

Role of Smartphones in IoT

Smartphones serve as an interface and command center for IoT devices, using in-built technologies like Wi-Fi, Bluetooth, NFC, GPS, and mobile networks (4G/5G) to communicate with smart devices.

Users can control and manage IoT devices remotely through specific mobile apps and cloud-based platforms. Smartphones also gather and process sensor data, offering customized and automated experiences.

Case Example: Smart Home Ecosystem

A smart home is one illustration of IoT integration with smartphones, where individuals can manage a variety of connected devices through mobile apps. In a home with the following devices that are IoT-enabled:

- **Smart Thermostat (e.g., Nest, Ecobee):** Regulates temperature according to user settings and weather, managed through a smartphone app.
- **Smart Lighting (e.g., Philips Hue, LIFX):** Enables users to turn lights on/off, adjust brightness, and schedule settings remotely.
- **Smart Security Systems (e.g., Ring, Arlo, Nest Cam):** Offers real-time monitoring, motion detection notices, and remote camera feeds access.
- **Smart Locks (e.g., August, Yale, Schlage):** Offers keyless entry and smartphone-controlled remote locking and unlocking.
- **Voice Assistants (e.g., Google Assistant, Alexa, Siri):** Seamlessly integrates with IoT devices and controls them via voice commands.

Automations, real-time notices, and AI-based suggestions are made available to users through mobile apps, which improve convenience, security, and *energy efficiency*.

Applications Outside Smart Homes

Healthcare & Wearables: Smartwatches and fitness bands (e.g., Apple Watch, Fitbit) track heart rate, sleep, and activity, syncing with smartphones for health monitoring.

- **Industrial IoT (IIoT)**: Smartphones are used to remotely monitor factory equipment, carry out predictive maintenance, and manage supply chains using IoT-connected sensors.
- **Smart Cities**: Public infrastructure like traffic lights, parking systems, and environmental monitors is controlled through smartphone-connected IoT networks.
- **Connected Vehicles**: Smartphones connect with IoT-enabled vehicles for remote diagnosis, GPS location, and infotainment system management.

Challenges and Security Issues

Though advantageous, smartphone-IoT integration is threatened by challenges such as data privacy threats, cyber threats, interoperability problems, and power consumption limitations. Cyberattacks on IoT devices pose a risk to user privacy and security. Data security is facilitated through encryption, multi-factor authentication, and blockchain technology. IoT ecosystems also need to embrace standardized protocols to make them communicate freely across different devices and manufacturers.

Future Prospects

With developments in 5G, AI, and edge computing, smartphone-IoT convergence is poised to become even more streamlined, providing quicker real-time processing, better automation, and AI-powered predictive analytics. Increased use of smart wearables, autonomous systems, and industrial IoT solutions will also fuel the uptake of smartphone-based IoT control, making life smarter and more interconnected.

SUMMARY

The evolution of multimedia big data computing in the context of IoT has changed real-time precision agriculture with monitoring, analytics, and automated decision-making capabilities. Such systems also improve the effciencies of remote sensing in IoT based smart cities and healthcare. The H.322 standard is critical to multimedia as it specifies the protocol stack and the procedures to set up a call. The Session Initiation Protocol (SIP) is used to manage multimedia sessions. It is a complex protocol with components, messages, and operations that communicate with one another. MGCP and RSVP as well as SIP with Session Description Protocol (SDP) serve as supporting protocols to SIP. Scibus and S.100 define the necessary infrastructure for the data processing and transfer to be classified as multimedia. Various real life examples bring out this importance to Video conferencing, Military surveillance, Interactive TV, Video on demand, and Smartphones which all serve as case studies in digital communication, security, and the IoT.